Strategic POSITIONING

Paul Temporal

Strategic POSITIONING

CREATING GROWTH
GENERATING PROFITS
ACHIEVING PERFORMANCE

OXFORD
UNIVERSITY PRESS

OXFORD
UNIVERSITY PRESS

4 Jalan Pemaju U1/15, Seksyen U1, 40150 Shah Alam,
Selangor Darul Ehsan, Malaysia

Oxford University Press is a department of the University of Oxford.
It furthers the University's objective of excellence in research, scholarship,
and education by publishing worldwide in

Oxford New York

Athens Auckland Bangkok Bogotá Buenos Aires Calcutta
Cape Town Chennai Dar es Salaam Delhi Florence Hong Kong Istanbul
Karachi Kuala Lumpur Madrid Melbourne Mexico City Mumbai
Nairobi Paris São Paulo Singapore Taipei Tokyo Toronto Warsaw

with associated companies in Berlin Ibadan

Oxford is a registered trade mark of Oxford University Press
in the UK and in certain other countries

Published in the United States
by Oxford University Press, New York

© Oxford University Press 1999
First published 1999

All rights reserved. No part of this publication may be reproduced,
stored in a retrieval system, or transmitted, in any form or by any means,
without the prior permission in writing of Oxford University Press.
Within Malaysia, exceptions are allowed in respect of any fair dealing for the
purpose of research or private study, or criticism or review, as permitted
under the Copyright Act currently in force. Enquiries concerning
reproduction outside these terms and in other countries should be
sent to Oxford University Press at the address above

This book is sold subject to the condition that it shall not, by way
of trade or otherwise, be lent, resold, hired out or otherwise circulated
without the publisher's prior consent in any form of binding or cover
other than that in which it is published and without a similar condition
including this condition being imposed on the subsequent purchaser

British Library Cataloguing in Publication Data
Data available

Library of Congress Cataloging-in-Publication Data
Temporal, Paul.
Strategic positioning: creating growth, generating profits, achieving high
performance/Paul Temporal
p. cm.
Includes index.
ISBN 983 56 0058 9
1. Corporations—Growth. 2. Strategic planning.
3. Industrial management. I. Title.
HD2746. T46 2000
658.4' 012—dc21
99-30913
CIP

Typeset by Indah Photosetting Centre Sdn. Bhd., Malaysia
Printed by Printmate Sdn. Bhd., Kuala Lumpur
Published by Penerbit Fajar Bakti Sdn. Bhd. (008974-T)
under licence from Oxford University Press

To my Mother and Father

Acknowledgements

THE ideas in this book are the result of my many years of work in the area of strategic marketing, branding, and positioning. I would like to thank the many clients I have worked with over the years for the opportunities they have given me, and for what they have taught me—for we all learn from our experiences—especially those whose names appear in the text.

There are others too who have shared their experiences, given me valuable insights, helped me crystallize my thoughts, and by so doing made this book a reality. In particular, I would like to thank Paddy Bowie for her constant help and support, Graham Bauer, Rod Davies, and Jeff Orr for their many ideas, Harry Alder, my co-author in the book *Corporate Charisma*, for his advice, and Beldev Singh for his final touches.

I would never have made it without the patience and tolerance of my family, Evelyn and Maria, who on many occasions must have felt very neglected.

To all of you and to the countless other persons who have helped me along the way—my deepest gratitude.

Contents

Acknowledgements	*vii*
Figures	*xii*
Introduction	*xiii*

1 Strategic Positioning Power — 1
Securing 'Piece of Mind' — 3
Managing Perceptions — 4
Taking Charge with Strategic Positioning — 6
Vision, Mission, and Strategic Positioning — 7
Personality, Values, Image, and Positioning — 10

2 Strategic Positioning For All — 13
What is Strategic Positioning — 15
Strategic Positioning Works for Everyone and Everything — 15
Strategic Positioning and the Self-concept — 22
The Strategic Positioning Process — 24
The Benefits and Rewards of Strategic Positioning — 27

3 Positioning Strategies — 29
Thirteen Positioning Strategies — 31
Gaining Power from Combining Positioning Strategies — 48
Capturing Hearts and Minds with Strategic Positioning — 49
Points to Remember When Choosing a Positioning Strategy — 50
Case Study — 51

4 Repositioning — 53
Repositioning — 55
Repositioning the Competition — 64
Multiple Repositioning — 65
Revolutionary Versus Evolutionary Positioning — 66
Case Studies in Repositioning — 68

5 Positioning and Branding — 71
Branding — 73
Brand Power and Positioning Power — 80
Case Study — 102

6 Positioning with Focus — 105
World Market Trends Affecting Positioning — 107
Giving Focus to Strategic Positioning — 112
Market Segmentation and Positioning — 115
Mass Customization, Segmentation, and Focused Marketing — 122
Case Study — 123

7 Strategic Positioning and Marketing Communications — 125
Positioning Statements — 127
Developing Key Messages for Different Audiences — 130
Total Communications for Strategic Positioning — 132
Tag Lines in Positioning — 144
Employing Agencies or Doing It Yourself — 145
Case Study — 149

8 Positioning and the Search for Success — 151
Perceptual Mapping — 153
Focus Groups — 155
Combining Quantitative and Qualitative Research for Strategic Positioning — 157
Monitoring and Protecting the Position — 169

9 Issues in Strategic Positioning — 171
The Repositioning of Nations — 173
Positioning and Country of Origin: Problems and Opportunities — 177

Global and Local Positioning Decisions: Getting
   the Right Balance   *180*
International Positioning: Some
   Considerations   *183*
Tough Choices in Positioning Technology   *184*
The Intimate Future: The Trend from Relationship
   Marketing to the Segment of One   *188*
Positioning in Times of Adversity   *197*

10 Strategic Positioning: Points to Ponder   *201*
Image Development and Protection   *203*
Strategic Positioning: Ten Points to Remember   *208*

Index   *209*

Figures

2.1	The Basic Positioning Process	*24*
2.2	Positioning and Image: The Virtuous Circle	*27*
3.1	The Thirteen Positioning Strategies	*31*
5.1	Building a Strong Brand Platform	*77*
5.2	Differentiation Through Strategic Positioning	*82*
5.3	The Power Grid	*100*
8.1	Example of a Perceptual Map	*159*
8.2	Perceptual Map with Price Attribute Overlay Using Regression Techniques	*160*
8.3	A Consumer Preference Map	*162*
8.4	Example of the Fit Between Image and the Self-concept of Consumers	*165*
9.1	International Positioning: Shifts in Age Group Attitudes	*184*

Introduction

HAVE YOU EVER WONDERED ...

How the corporate giants achieve their strength?
What makes some companies and products so much more successful than others?
How companies can move into new industries with apparent ease?
How companies and products can appeal to every national culture?
What attracts people to buy famous but very expensive brands?
Why the number one companies and brands of seventy years ago are still in the top spot today?
How companies develop brand equity that adds billions of dollars to their saleable assets?
How ordinary products and services get out of the commodity trap and appear different from the rest?
What it takes to increase customer acquisition and loyalty?
How the value is added in 'value added' marketing?
How you can read minds through research?
How the 'supermarketeers' manage consumer perceptions?

The answers to all these questions have one thing in common—they involve strategic positioning techniques. Competitive strategy is very much concerned with being different, and strategic positioning is the way in which this is achieved. It is a subject often mentioned in business conversations, but widely misunderstood and misinterpreted. And despite its critical importance to the strategic marketing process, it receives no more than a cursory mention in the majority of management books. Those who have written about positioning in-depth are few and far between.

The truth about positioning is that it is ubiquitous, and can determine whether an enterprise fails or flourishes, because the end result of positioning is image. Everything an organization does (and sometimes omits to do) influences people's view of it, sometimes leaving them feeling indifferent, but more usually influencing their feelings in a positive or negative way. Public perceptions—in other words the image they have of an organization—can influence how successful or unsuccessful it will be. A poor image can damage stock price, give rise to adverse reports and ratings by analysts, make fund-raising difficult, increase pressure from shareholders, lose customers, damage morale, and reduce profitability. A good image can lead to a sustainable competitive advantage and precisely the reverse of these negative effects.

Positioning at its simplest involves establishing a favourable opinion or image in people's minds. Organizations often do not realize that whether or not they have consciously attempted to gain a position, or establish an image, they already have one. Those that research on their image are often disappointed in what they find. Few understand that they can influence people's perceptions through positioning techniques and actions and by so doing control and shape their image and destiny. Despite the close association with the commercial world, image management applies just as much to individuals, non-profit-making enterprises, government departments and agencies, and even nations. They all need to manage their image because adverse perceptions can lead to failure, and good perceptions can bring success to all.

This book is about strategic positioning and how to harness its power. Positioning is strategic and should not be treated as a tactical marketing tool. It is a strategic weapon because it can make the difference between the ordinary and the élite, and because it requires the realignment of organizational resources and activities to do so. Like any strategy, it is long term in nature but the outcome of successful strategic positioning is a powerful image. Indeed, because positioning can produce such spectacular results as those mentioned above, I have called this book *Strategic Positioning*.

The text takes you through the strategic positioning process, and the various techniques associated with it. Based on the most up-to-date methods used by world-class companies, the skills of strategic positioning are presented in practical step-by-step method and illustrated by examples and cases from many industries, markets, and situations.

Chapter 1 outlines the basic ideas behind strategic positioning, especially the importance of managing people's perceptions, and shows how they link to image, personality, values, visions and missions, and success.

Chapter 2 explains strategic positioning in more detail. Anything and anyone can be positioned powerfully. Here I describe the four basic stages of the positioning process and then discuss some of the results that strategic positioning can achieve.

Chapter 3 looks at the various choices or strategies available in strategic positioning, and how they can be combined for maximum success. This is the 'powerhouse' or the engine-room if you like. Choosing the right strategy will determine the outcome.

Chapter 4 covers in depth the reasons why repositioning takes place, and how it is achieved.

Chapter 5 looks at brands and brand building, and the strategic positioning techniques you can use whether for a company, product, or person. You will also discover in this chapter how a brand can occupy one or more positions. Finally, I explain how you can gain maximum impact from strategic positioning in terms of brand loyalty and the customer experience.

Chapter 6 looks at targets. It is no use giving the right messages to the wrong people. Strategic positioning demands focus and identifying exactly your target audience. I discuss market segmentation techniques in detail, with particular emphasis on the newer psychographic approaches.

Chapter 7 deals with executional issues. I cover particularly the subject of how to write a good positioning statement and how to choose the appropriate media to communicate the right messages, such as advertising, promotions, and public relations. Special emphasis is given to the importance of integrating emotion into positioning so as to add power.

Chapter 8 looks at how to measure positioning success and the research techniques, such as focus groups, that have been found to be of most use. These include perceptual mapping, which visually gives you a view of where you are versus the competition in people's minds, which is an essential tool for creating powerful positions.

Chapter 9 discusses some topical issues of interest, including strategic positioning for nations, the problems and opportunities arising from country of origin, global and local strategic positioning decisions, the very real problems of influencing people's minds about technology and technology products, and the role of positioning in the advances made by relationship marketing.

Chapter 10 summarizes the strategic positioning process by offering a step-by-step question guide for anyone who has responsibilities for building a strong or stronger image.

WHO THIS BOOK IS FOR

Many books deal with concepts, and explain them well, but fail to show people how they can successfully implement the ideas. This book is written from a practical point of view. Consequently, it will appeal to all those people who want to know how to get others to see themselves or their organizations differently, and build up a powerful image. As strategic positioning is also a widely applicable package of ideas and techniques, it will therefore be of interest to a wide range of people, including:
- Chief Executive Officers and General Managers
- Marketing Directors and Managers
- Brand, Category, and Product Development Managers
- Advertising, Promotion, and Public Relations Specialists
- Corporate Affairs and Corporate Communications Managers
- Corporate Planners and Business Development Specialists
- Marketing and Communications Consultants
- Those who work in Government Ministries and Departments who have to deal with media and communications
- Students of Business and Communications
- And of course, anyone who wants to build their own image, including politicians, business people, entrepreneurs, and entertainers

How This Book Will Help You

You will find this book of assistance in helping you to:
- Achieve your vision and mission
- Build and manage a strong brand and/or corporate image
- Make your company appear different and better than the competition
- Choose and implement the right strategies to create and maintain a unique, powerful image
- Reposition and turn around your business
- Focus your total marketing effort for maximum impact
- Influence and manage the perceptions of key target audiences
- Attract and retain more customers
- Employ up-to-date research techniques to analyse and improve your competitive stance
- Save and get more for your money from advertising and promotion

So, whoever you are, whatever your business is, or whatever the size of your organization, if you want to change people's views, attitudes, and perceptions, this book will help you do it. Above all, it will help you achieve results.

Strategic Positioning Power

Securing 'Piece of Mind'

When you want to get to know someone, you go out of your way to get yourself in their sights—to meet them, talk to them, to get them to notice you, to acknowledge you, and ultimately to like you. In a room full of people this can present difficulties, so you need carefully planned ways of getting through to them. For instance, you edge closer, or talk to someone who might know him or her. Sometimes, you need to do something unexpected to get noticed, to show you are different and deserve their precious attention. Once you have caught their attention, to really get them to like you, they need to like you as a personality, want to see more of you, and want to be sure you are sincere, consistent, and dependable. You need to earn their friendship over a period of time, and to show yourself as different and better than others who want to occupy a special place in their minds.

That is not easy. People can be suspicious, wary of strangers, and do not like being pushed. Besides, many do not like change. They tend to prefer things the way they are, and will get angry if you are aggressive, bored if you are dull and uninteresting. If you are neutral so are they. The sorts of thoughts that go through their minds are

> Why are they looking at me?
> What does he want?
> Is she pressuring me?
> Why are they so pushy?
> He's just the same as everyone else!
> He only wants one thing!
> They are after my money!
> Why should I trust them?
> I'm not sure whether she is my type!
> He does not seem as nice as . . .
> and so on.

We are familiar with these sorts of thoughts. We may have wondered, 'How can I get through to her?' 'How can I win him over?' 'How can I boost my image?' We have all had to compete with others and show someone somehow that we are special in some way.

It is the same for companies and even nations. The buzzword 'hypercompetition' is not an overstatement. People and organizations compete for the attention of increasingly sophisticated listeners and consumers. It is hard to get heard let alone establish a relationship. The 'noise' in the marketplace 'room' is horrendous. The clutter of advertising, events, as well as promotional activities and the proliferation of media communications make it so much more difficult to get messages through, to find that 'piece of mind' that we look for to secure that powerful image we want.

From book publishing to banking, cars to computers, fast food to fashion, music to medicine, politics to pharmaceutical goods, technology to tourism—whatever business you are in, it is getting harder and harder to get a share of voice, a share of mind, a share of the future.

How can you overcome this problem? How can you outperform all the others in the market-place? How can you show that you are different and better? How can you stand out in the crowd? How can you capture people's imagination and turn interest into long lasting friendship? How can you squeeze in and survive? How can you make a truly lasting impression? How can you develop a powerful position in people's minds?

This book will show you how, and much more.

It will also relate all that is said to different industries and situations, so that from the many examples given you will gain practical value and be able to apply the concepts in your own situation. As a practitioner rather than an academic you need to know how to implement these ideas. But first of all we should look at how to start to gain that 'piece of mind'. To do this we need techniques to successfully influence or manage people's *perceptions*.

Managing Perceptions

Minds are powerful things, and changing people's minds is a difficult task. Whenever anyone is introduced in any way to anything for any length of time they immediately form a view of it in their mind—*a perception*. The word *percept* is 'a recognizable sensation or impression received by the mind through the senses'. The word *perception* is defined in *Webster's Dictionary* as

1. '(a) the act of perceiving or the ability to perceive; mental grasp of objects, qualities etc. by means of the senses; awareness; comprehension; (b) insight or intuition, or the facility for these.'
2. 'The understanding, knowledge etc., gotten by perceiving, or a specific idea, concept, impression etc. so formed.'

Because perceptions are automatic—the mind forms them whether we like them and want them or not—they play an important role in our everyday lives and the decisions we make. Positive perceptions lead to positive actions and vice versa. The word *position* can be defined as 'the place where a person or a thing is especially in relation to others' and 'a creation or condition in which one has the advantage'.

The link between perception and position is that, according to scientific research, when someone perceives something it is stored in the mind in a certain 'position'. Usually this 'position' stores other information about similar things in a similar storage space and automatically compares them against each other. So when we meet someone, we immediately form a view of them and store them automatically in the mental position labelled 'I like him and I like him more than X because ...'.

This is just a simplification of a complex mental process. The mind, as we all know, is much more adept at storing and retrieving data than the best of today's supercomputers, and it can store up to millions (or even billions) of perceptions, allocating them to various 'positions' in the brain. The brain has a more or less infinite perceptual space within which everything we experience is at first placed, compared with other things, and either discarded (forgotten) or kept (remembered). It is like a huge complicated filing system. Because of the large number of items stored certain files are kept active when communications concerning them are occurring and there is interest, whereas files that are 'dead' are placed out of sight and consequently out of mind. To get a favourable file spot and gain a good perception, what is communicated must be good. To keep that filing space active, meaningful communication must continue. To get out of the 'dead' files area we need to secure a change of mind that places us in a more important category and which generates more interest. So positions are like files, and good perceptions are good filing spots at the front of people's minds.

SELECTIVE PERCEPTION

It is difficult to get a good position or filing spot in people's minds because they only accept a tiny proportion of all the information and messages they receive. This is sometimes referred to as selective perception, because people have to sort out what is important to them from all the thousands of pieces of information they are bombarded with every day. The task for strategic positioning is to make sure that the communications you send are good enough to, first of all, get noticed, and then, appear relevant enough to fit in with their needs and warrant further investigation. They also have to be superior to all the many competitor messages targeting them.

TAKING CHARGE WITH STRATEGIC POSITIONING

If there is one point worth remembering it is this: unless it is completely new to people whom you wish to influence, you will already have a position in their minds, no matter who you are, or whatever company, product, or concept you represent. Therefore, it is better to take the initiative and try to control or shape people's perceptions rather than let them develop them in an uncontrolled fashion.

If we seek to influence consumer opinion, we need to address two questions. First, how can we achieve a positive perception which leads to a strong position in the minds of people we want to influence, when there are thousands of other people, products, and companies clamouring to do the same? Second, if a perception of us is already there, but is not as favourable as we want it to be, how can we change people's minds about us, and gain a better position relative to those with whom we are competing?

This is the job of strategic positioning—to gain and hold a strong position and a favourable perception in people's minds. The word *strategic* is added here to underline the fact that any attempt to do this must be carefully thought through, and be linked to the goals or objectives we wish to achieve—whether to build more sales, create a stronger image, gain a competitive advantage, or whatever else we have in mind.

Strategic positioning seeks to manage perceptions, to get people to think of us in a certain way, and to keep us in a strong position in their minds. This is no easy task, but this book will reveal a variety of powerful and proven techniques used by top companies and personalities around the world. By reading it you will become a master practitioner of strategic positioning.

Vision, Mission, and Strategic Positioning

A vision statement is an expression of long-term goals. It is a guide for the future; an aspirational destination that is highly motivational. Sometimes, corporate, personal, or national visions might be more like dreams than burning ambitions. Nevertheless, as long as a vision is motivating and not totally unrealistic it will serve its purpose. A vision must be achievable to a large extent.

With companies it often describes strategic intent as opposed to financial objectives. Most companies express their visions in vision statements while others use slogans, and they can differ a great deal. Some are very general in nature; for example Toyota's vision is encapsulated in the slogan 'To Win' and Motorola's in its 'Total Customer Satisfaction'. Vtech's vision is to use the latest technology available to produce high quality, innovative, brand-name products that are better than anything else on the market. Others are more specific, as is the case with Permodalan Nasional Berhad's 'We will be a world class investment organization, distinctive and successful in everything we do'. As the purpose of a vision statement is to express aspirations and goals in a motivating way, it could be argued that being highly specific really does not matter.

However, as they should be easily understood, vision statements are better if they are simple to say and recall. BSN Commercial Bank has the vision of becoming 'The Heartbeat of the Community'. This is simple, memorable, and a good summary of its intention to be not just another bank, but to play a genuine part in the growth and activities of the local communities within which it operates. But much more than a public statement, the vision is supported by many projects carried out to help create wealth in local, regional, and national communities.

But visions and vision statements are not the sole prerogative of companies—they can be equally useful for nations and individuals. Malaysia, for example, has a 'Vision 2020', the brainchild of Prime Minister Mahathir Mohamad, and which encapsulates the date by which the country aspires to become a fully developed nation. It has motivated everyone in the country to a high degree, and is a key driver for the government and all sectors of the population. Go to the smallest village in the most rural parts of Malaysia and everyone knows what 'Vision 2020' means. This is an example of an individual offering a vision of the future for a country. But individuals must have their own visions too. As is often said, if you do not know where you want to go, it is unlikely you will get there. A young career diplomat on the fast track, for instance, may have a vision of being a top-ranking ambassador within twenty to twenty-five years, or a salesperson may set a long-term goal of becoming marketing manager for a major group of companies within ten years. A young person learning music might aspire to become a world-class concert pianist. Each has a personal vision that drives him or her on to success.

If vision statements describe where a company or a person intends to go or be, mission statements tend to mark out the route by describing how to get there. For Motorola, the mission statement that added specificity to its vision statement was its six-sigma quality programme, which meant tolerating only 3.4 manufacturing defects per million. Missions tend to be more specific and shorter term in nature, more present than future oriented. Even though specificity is important, mission statements are also best kept to a few highly significant words so that people can understand and remember them. Disney's mission—'To Make People Happy'—is a great example, with every aspect of human resource development and management totally geared up to making it happen every day.

More often than not companies have either or both of the vision and mission statements in black and white, sometimes combined into one statement. Nations also have agendas that fit these categories. In fact we all have some dream or goal that we want to achieve. What is normally lacking, however, is the crispness, clarity, and accuracy of our objective. It is important to have a written vision, mission, or goal specifying what is to be achieved.

HOW POSITIONING HELPS

Strategic positioning is a very important ingredient in the realization of any vision and/or mission, because it provides focus and motivation. It looks not from the inside out (like vision and mission) but from the outside in. It describes how we want to be perceived by other people, and does this in a way that differentiates us from every other company or person. In this way, it can be of great value in vision and mission creation. Conversely, if vision and mission statements possess a customer focus, then it is easier to see where positioning fits as a strategy for their achievement. For example, when expressing its vision, computer software company Logica says, 'We know our customers seek business understanding, flexibility, high quality people and service, and value for money.' Such a clear and precise statement of customer expectations contains not only the direction for product and service development, but also the perceptual elements which, if satisfied, will create a powerful image. With clear, well-founded, customer-based information in a vision or mission statement, the foundation and focus for strategic positioning is not in doubt. Unfortunately, this is not often evident.

The positioning process also helps provide focus in another way, by treating different audiences differently and adopting key messages that will be particularly attractive to them. Different positions can be created for different customer groups, yet remain true to the perceived personality. This particular issue is discussed in more detail in Chapter 5.

Personality, Values, Image, and Positioning

PERSONALITY AND VALUES

We all want to look good. It is a human trait, a universal desire applicable to both people and organizations. We all want to have a good image, but whether we enjoy one or not depends partly on our personality, because personality is the basis of who we are and how we behave. It also depends partly on how we project ourselves to others. Personality is based largely on values such as a belief in being honest (shared values if it involves more than one person), and to some extent on personality traits or characteristics such as confidence. A corporate vision or a mission will provide direction, but like an ordinary person the company's actual behaviour will be shaped by its values and how its employees exhibit these.

Values are important because they have the potential to set apart one identity or person from another, especially as they often translate into firm and consistent behaviours. Values in individuals reveal what is most important to them, and values in companies do the same, telling staff and customers what behaviours are most important. They form the prevailing culture of a society or an organization that determines the kind of experience customers receive when they interact with it, and can prove to be a significant factor in differentiating it from competitors. Given that fact, it makes sense for companies to choose their values carefully, and demonstrate them on every possible occasion. As values largely determine personality, the correct choice of values by a company can be used to develop a truly likeable personality that can result in a very favourable image. Conversely, if a company merely allows its culture to develop in an *ad hoc* way, it may end up with a personality that customers are either indifferent to, or do not particularly like. No wonder that corporate cultures based on shared values are now confirmed as being a key ingredient for long-term success, and enlightened companies are building personalities based on them.

POSITIONING AND PERSONALITY

Basing a proposed positioning on the values of your company, your products, or yourself can be successful. Remaining true to certain values is fundamental to success in every field, and demonstrating those values consistently is important for the reputation and image of a personality. Mere performance is not enough, because others can emulate that. Positioning tells people your values and what they mean. Values that are lived out every day will help create a personality that cannot be copied. Positioning presents that personality to the world.

To ensure positioning success, your image should be built around and reinforced by those values. For instance, if one of your main or core values is dependability, it should become part of everyday behaviour (or culture for companies) as a personality trait. It should also become part of the key messages you communicate—why you are different and better. Your image will then be one of reliability of someone or something that can be depended on. You will then 'own' that position in people's minds. Personality strategies as a basis for positioning are discussed more fully in Chapter 3, and examples of how brand personalities are built are provided in Chapter 5.

STRATEGIC POSITIONING DEMANDS CREDIBILITY

Strategic positioning is therefore highly important in image building. First of all, strong positions are built by giving a target audience an opportunity to see something as it really is, and to show how it is different from or better than the others—it communicates uniqueness. Secondly, positioning influences minds. An image, be it of a person, place, nation, product, or company is just a collective summary of perceptions. Projecting certain characteristics of a 'person' can build an image by influencing how that 'person' is seen or perceived by others. One element of positioning is potentially dangerous: human perception can be based on fact or fiction. In other words, what you see in another person, or company, may not be necessarily true. For instance, someone might tell you that he is very trustworthy, but he is actually a thief. His outward presentation and the things he says portray a person of integrity—a hard-working professional in a steady job.

Underneath, however, he is really a person who preys on the weaknesses of others, and persuades them to invest in fictitious enterprises.

Another example: A manager of a music or film star builds an image, through skilful promotions, of a solid person who cares about others and does lots of charitable work— someone you would love to have in your family. The press, however, uncovers a violent, drug-dominated, private life—a dysfunctional personality. Similarly, a politician positions himself as the very antithesis of corruption, but is eventually found out to be more corrupt than most. A company says 'We are dedicated to customer service' but cannot ensure that telephones are answered promptly. Some people think it is easy to fool others by telling them how good they are so as to build up their image, but building positions that are not credible or sustainable increases vulnerability. So make sure you deliver on the promise. On the positive side, if you position yourself on a real strength, your image will grow and grow. Strategic positioning enhances the reality that is you, or your company, or product, because it draws upon the unique characteristics we all have.

Base your desired position on *real* strengths. There should be no difference between what you say and what you do. There should be no credibility gap. If a photo shop makes a promise in its advertising or promotion materials that developed film will be ready in one hour then it should be ready in an hour. Strategic positioning works when you can and do deliver on your promises.

In Chapter 2 you will find out more about strategic positioning and how it can help virtually anyone or anything, from products to places to politicians. You will also be introduced to an easy four-stage process that will help you to apply strategic positioning to your particular situation and bring the rewards you desire.

Strategic Positioning For All

What is Strategic Positioning?

Strategic positioning is a strategic initiative that convinces or persuades people to think about why you are better than and/or different from whatever your competitors have to offer. If done well it has compelling appeal. It differentiates the ordinary from the special in people's minds. It provides magnetic attraction that is hard to resist. For companies it can generate huge profits; for nations it can change media, political, and public opinion; for individuals it can deliver the breakthrough needed to acquire prestige, respect, success, and wealth.

Positioning depends on perceptions, and perceptions are the result of a filtering process. Whatever you say or communicate to people passes through 'filters' that affect the way in which they eventually think about it. This is why you often think you have said the right things but then find out that what people thought you said is quite different. And even if they check out all right, you sometimes find that they are forgotten all too easily. The messages therefore have to be powerful in themselves, and great care must be taken to ensure that they are not misinterpreted or forgotten. They must make long-lasting vivid impressions.

Strategic positioning selects the messages you send and the best means to send them. It ensures that people see the messages clearly, and that they have such great impact that they are not easily forgotten. But more than that, strategic positioning attracts minds and brings about positive actions in the thoughts and deeds of the target audience.

Strategic Positioning Works For Everyone and Everything

Positioning is applicable to every circumstance where influencing minds is the objective. Everything has a 'position' in that people who see or hear about them form views, judgements, comparisons, ratings, and opinions. Given the fact that people's thoughts and behaviours can be influenced, then strategic positioning can be used in a multitude of situations to help, for instance

- Politicians

- Countries and nations
- Non-profit organizations
- Places and destinations
- Entertainers
- Companies, products, and services
- Ordinary people

There actually is no limit to the variety of uses, as long as the principles are followed. Here are a few examples. More detailed ones will be given in later chapters to illustrate different parts of the process and the end results. The thing to remember is whoever you are, whatever you might be, however big or small you think your product or company is, whatever problem you have with your image, strategic positioning is there to help you.

STRATEGIC POSITIONING FOR POLITICIANS

Nowadays it is quite common for politicians to think marketing. Indeed, in some cases, rarely a speech is made, an event opened, a baby kissed, or a TV appearance scheduled without stringent analysis by 'spin doctors', public relations staff/consultants, or campaign managers (sometimes all the lot!). Many politicians are now turning to consultants and advisers to create and manage their desired images. Just like products and companies, they have highly structured marketing plans carefully thought out with respect to quantifiable goals and positions. Like those same things, they are packaged to attract the voters (customers) they want.

Politicians and those aspiring to high office are being advised on what identity they want to portray, and consequently how to position themselves for maximum impact. In the United States, the phrase 'high name ID' is used to describe the degree of public awareness the politician has— 90 per cent being desirable for big campaigns and polls. This is similar to brand awareness measures used by companies. 'Brand attitude' is a phrase used to describe the ratio of positives–negatives given by the public (4:1 being good) in relation to the politician concerned.

Among the successful are the campaigns which rocketed Margaret Thatcher to fame and revamped her image from that of someone appearing as fusty and old-fashioned to one more confident, modern, and authoritative. Nothing was spared from hairstyle and make-up to enunciation, dressing, and body language. The result was not just national but international fame. Of course, we must not underestimate the effects of policy decisions and the odd bit of luck like the Falklands War, which helped to increase Thatcher's image. But no one can deny that the public relations people did a great job. Other politicians have also used strategic positioning principles to achieve success, such as George Bush in his campaign against Michael Dukakis, and Tony Blair in bringing the Labour party back in from the cold. Political power depends entirely on how well those who seek it can manage the perceptions of their audiences better than their competitors. This can only be accomplished by skilful positioning.

STRATEGIC POSITIONING FOR COUNTRIES AND NATIONS

Countries are world brands in their own right. By their very existence (and this is true for the majority of countries, particularly developed ones) they have a global *identity*. Whether they do anything positive or not in projecting that identity, certain messages go out to the rest of the world, and the rest of the world comes to hold a certain view about them. In other words, they also have an *image*. In this respect they are no different from other mega brands associated with global companies and products such as Coca-Cola. They have ubiquitous awareness but are perceived in many different ways by various groups of people.

It is primarily image that concerns countries, because of patriotism, politics, and economics. Everyone wants his or her country to be seen in the best light. However, where a company would make a huge effort to manage its image by managing the perceptions of its target consumers, countries have, for the most part, allowed their images to evolve in an *ad hoc* way. It is in this respect that they can learn much from the world of corporate positioning. A full discussion of positioning nations and countries is given in Chapter 9.

STRATEGIC POSITIONING FOR NON-PROFIT ORGANIZATIONS

A few years ago it was rare to find non-profit organizations advertising in the mass media. Nowadays it is commonplace. Organizations such as CARE, UNICEF, and even the Boy Scouts have recently mounted advertising campaigns designed to create more awareness, and boost their respective images. The need for funding is the problem, and organizations of this nature are now jockeying for position in the minds of those who have the capability to donate money for worthy causes, whether they be governments, corporations, or individuals. They are using the positioning process to attract the attention of donors and supporters, and persuading them that they are different from the competition, and worthy of attention. Image advertising is the result of carefully thought out positioning strategies.

STRATEGIC POSITIONING FOR PLACES AND DESTINATIONS

Places, cities, or holiday destinations, for instance, can also be positioned strongly in people's minds. There is a lovely virtually unspoilt island off the coast of Malaysia called Pangkor Laut that is positioned so well to attract people who are looking for exclusivity and pure natural surroundings—with some gorgeous advertising shots that make you want to jump on a plane immediately. The tag line 'One Island, One Resort' sums it all up. It is memorable, it is different, and it is desirable. Strategic positioning creates desire.

The Docklands in London provide another example. Once regarded as belonging to the last century—run-down, dilapidated, and not in the least desirable for anyone—the new positioning has attracted big business and the rich and famous. It's amazing what strategic positioning can do!

What both these examples do is demonstrate that it is not the actual place that matters (the world has millions) but the attractions that can be presented and positioned skilfully in the minds of potential customers. What's the attraction to stop over at Dubai? A dream luxury car in the duty-free draw for one in every 1000 people. The positioning is expressed in these tag lines: 'Dubai duty free drives the world'—'Fly, Buy, Dubai.'

Why is Disneyland on the 'wish' list of millions of families? Because it is positioned so powerfully as the best total entertainment experience in the world. The combination of fantasy, thrills, famous characters, and pure fun within the Magic Kingdom is presented as a lifetime family experience. Disneyland says it will make you and your family happy, and it delivers on the promise.

Strategic positioning for places is no longer a luxury; it is a necessity. Consumers are faced with a bewildering amount of choices in destinations they can visit, and falling travel costs make it increasingly difficult for marketeers to attract visitors to their locations. The marketing of places is fast becoming a commodity business, and only those who are capable of applying the best positioning techniques will convince people that their destinations are different and better than all the other available and highly advertised choices.

STRATEGIC POSITIONING FOR ENTERTAINERS

Moving from places of entertainment to a smaller scale, it still pays to concentrate on target audience perceptions. With individual entertainers, for instance, there are thousands of comedians, rock groups, magicians, and singers, but strategic positioning can make the difference and a person can own something that is difficult for the competition to take away. For those who grew up in the 1960s and 1970s, the words 'surfing songs' brings to mind the Beach Boys. Michael Jackson is positioned as the King of Pop and millions really believe it. Mention magicians and David Copperfield is right there in people's minds. How do they achieve this top-of-the-mind recall? How do other well-known celebrities like Larry King and Jay Leno develop images that create huge viewer followings? The answer is that they have positioned themselves (or, more often than not, have been positioned) so well that to their viewers they have no equal. Of course, they have to perform consistently well, just as a product has to do if sales are to be maintained. However, the difference comes not so much from performance, but from a carefully crafted image, the result of strategic positioning. In this respect, there is little difference between globally successful products and the stars of entertainment. They are all basically commodities that have been built into strong brands.

The usefulness of strategic positioning for people in the entertainment business is that it is the only way for them to break away from the crowd, and generate mass appeal. There are probably many more people in those fields who could perform to a similar standard, but if you look at those who achieve 'stardom' you will see that they have been marketed very cleverly, and have developed unique images, even though they might not possess outstanding talent. They are often (but not always) just ordinary people when compared to others in their chosen fields, except that they have had the strategic positioning treatment and it works.

So successful is the attraction built up for celebrities, that psychologists are declaring that people are becoming addicted to them, just like the addictions some people have for items such as cigarettes, liquor, and chocolate. The more they see the celebrities, the more they want them, and any misdemeanours that they happen to commit seem almost to add to the entertainment, so strong are the associations that exist in the minds of fans. They develop virtual intimate relationships with these celebrities, and the positioning experts reinforce their fantasies with well-planned media coverage, public appearances, and event-driven exposure.

STRATEGIC POSITIONING FOR COMPANIES, PRODUCTS, AND SERVICES

There are plenty of examples of strategic positioning for companies, products, and services in the later sections of the book, but without fail, all of the major successes around the world have built themselves powerful positions in the minds of customers. Here are two examples.

Throughout this century Rolls Royce cars have constantly been regarded as the ultimate luxury vehicle. There has always been and still is world acceptance of this view. The strategic positioning of Rolls Royce based on quality and craftsmanship—the very best—has never been overtaken by any rival. The interesting challenge for Rolls Royce cars in the next few years is whether the company can maintain perceptions that its top quality products associated with the best of Britain can still be the same under foreign ownership. Strategic positioning is based on factual or non-factual perceptions, as we know. Adjustments such as a new foreign corporate owner could change perceptions of the final product *even if nothing else changed at all* in terms of product quality and superiority. Strategic positioning determines image and image, being fragile, has to be looked after very carefully. This complex area of brand associations and image is discussed further in Chapter 5.

Some individual products have developed such powerful positions that people use their brand names as generic descriptions of a whole industry product range. In some countries of the world, for instance, when people say they are going to buy some Colgate they mean toothpaste and not necessarily the Colgate brand. In these circumstances, when an individually branded product mentally represents the generic product it is not surprising that market shares reach 60 to 80 per cent proportions. That is strategic positioning, and it can give you sustainable market leadership.

Would you rather take a train journey through Europe on a normal train or on the Orient Express? Would you rather fly in a jumbo jet or the Concorde? Product quality and performance spell the difference, but the premiums charged represent not only that but also other associations in the minds of consumers—status, mystery, romance, prestige. These associations appear in people's minds *because they have been deliberately positioned as such*.

STRATEGIC POSITIONING FOR ORDINARY PEOPLE

Strategic positioning can work for anyone who wants to change how other people view them. Wearing a suit makes some people feel different and confident, so they act how they feel. This happens because the associations of success and their mental image of successful business people relate to high standards of self-presentation. So the very act of dressing well raises self-esteem, and actually can give the impression of success to those who observe it. One (now famous) salesman in the United States was down on his luck. He had made hundreds of sales calls even to his friends and lost the contracts he was hoping they would give him. His last desperate acts were to rent a limousine, actually refuse meetings with friends when they phoned to see him socially saying he was too busy with work, and buy a new suit. He nearly went broke doing it but his friends thought 'Hey, he is doing well! Great! I must call him again. Maybe he can do something for me?' He never looked back and now he is a rich man. So seeing can be believing, and perception need not be based on fact. It is what you say and do and how you say and do it. That is strategic positioning.

If you are going for a job interview, the two things you have to convince the interviewers of are why you are better than other candidates (what you can do better than others), and why you are different (what you can do that others cannot). Anyone who can persuade people to think that they are different and better will enhance their image and beat the competition.

Strategic Positioning and The Self-concept

People like people, and they tend to like people who are similar to them. People in organizations recruit people like themselves. People try to influence other people to be like themselves. Everyone has his or her own concept of what he or she is, or would like to be, and what he or she wants other people to recognize them as being. This self-concept or self-ideal—if we can discover it—provides a basis of how we can appeal to other's conscious and subconscious minds and give them what they are looking for, be it a friend, an icon, a point of reference, or anything else they can relate to. We can also use self-concept as a measurement of how successful our positioning has been, as shown in Chapter 8.

An everyday example of how the self-concept works is in the hospitality industry—basically an industry which provides people with places to eat, drink, and sleep in, whether it be for business or pleasure. When someone makes a decision to go to a place of hospitality—a hotel, a restaurant, a bar, or any combination of the three—that decision will be influenced to a great extent by the person's needs for association or expression. Apart from the obvious needs and wants (food, drink, and sleep) and even taking into account budgetary constraints, there are other factors influential in the decision-

making process. For instance, the need to:
- Be with people of similar backgrounds
- Express oneself and impress others
- Maintain a certain lifestyle
- Reinforce and reward oneself
- Achieve certain goals or aspirations

In other words, their self-concept comes into play. Understanding what self-concepts people have gives us the edge in influencing their thoughts and gaining a strong positioning in their minds, and we can gear our products and services to try to satisfy these psychological self-concept needs.

Although advertising and promotion undoubtedly influence people's thoughts, positioning can also be enhanced by theming the product to reinforce the desired image and appeal to the self-concept of consumers. Some of the 'product features' you can alter to position places of entertainment in relation to self-concept are:
- External features and location
- Interior design
- Attitudes of staff
- Staff attire
- Product range and prices
- Name, logo, and tag line
- Ambience

These, when combined with promotional activities, can draw in certain types of customers. Successful establishments, elegant surroundings, and a certain type of customer base might attract people with high self-esteem. Positioning tools here might be up-market brochures to describe the experience people will have, and reveal a luxurious or exclusive ambience. News coverage of a VIP or celebrity visit, and power words in the media such as 'sheer luxury' will all help get the message across. Saying you are the most expensive place in town can be good for egocentric and aspirational customers. Copy like 'Just for once in your life treat yourself to the best' can entice the 'wannabes' to come or those who want to reward themselves. The local pub serving food appeals to people who want a sociable atmosphere and not have to cook. At the other end of the market, a family-oriented person just wants value for money and a favourite fun experience for their kids, so companies like McDonald's provide play areas, merchandise, and other attractions to complete the experience—a family lifestyle.

It all depends on what you want to do and whom you want to target. The success then rests on how well the enterprise is positioned, and how well it is supported by the experience.

THE STRATEGIC POSITIONING PROCESS

FOUR BASIC STEPS

Briefly there are four basic elements or steps involved in strategic positioning. At this stage these will be explained quite simply, but in the last chapter of the book, these steps are divided into separate areas with questions to consider when working through the whole positioning process. They are:

- Step 1: Know where you are
- Step 2: Know where you want to be
- Step 3: Take action to get there
- Step 4: Decide whether you have achieved your desired position.

Figure 2.1 shows the four basic steps in positioning, and emphasises that it is really a continuous process, which must be continually monitored and adjusted depending on market and competitive changes.

FIGURE 2.1
The Basic Positioning Process

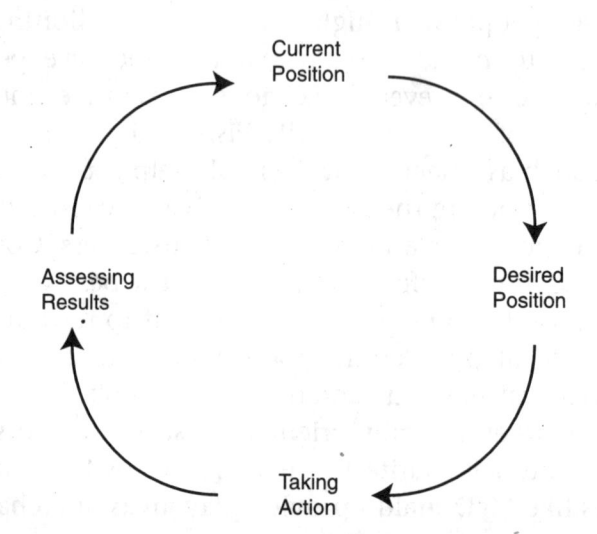

STEP 1: Know Where You Are—Establish Your Current Position

Sometimes companies and people have a feeling in their minds that something is not right but they are not entirely sure what it is. For instance, a new product is not selling, customer complaints have risen alarmingly, or someone thinks they are not getting anywhere in achieving their goals. Such feelings need exploration. If it is personal, ask your friends. If it is your company or product, ask your customers. If you are in the entertainment business, ask your fans. But ask! Do some research, whether informal or formal, internal or externally commissioned. As the main output of strategic positioning is *image* find out what the current image is. What do people like about it? What do people not like about it? Where do they think you can improve? If you represent a country and your tourism figures are going down, ask travellers and travel agents. If your political ratings are down, ask some voters or lobbyists. If you employ staff and/or advisers ask them too, because the truth is often closer than you think. If you do not ask and you do not know where you stand, you are likely to take actions that are inappropriate and potentially damaging. Finally, never forget your competitors. If your image is in a downswing theirs might be in an upswing, and you need to know why.

Some kind of research is vital, and some techniques for this are elaborated on in Chapter 8.

STEP 2: Know Where You Want To Be—Establish Your Desired Position

Once you have gone through Step 2, you will have some idea of where you want to be but you need to set clear goals. For individuals and organizations this usually involves answering these questions:
- What do you want to know?
- What do you want to do?
- What do you want to have or get?
- What do you want to be?
- What do you want to achieve in terms of relationships?

The answers may be qualitative or quantitative in nature. For instance, over the next three years a bank might want to move from having a 4 per cent to a 10 per cent share of the market for housing loans to the Yuppies. Step 1 has revealed that currently the image of the bank in the minds of the desired new market is one of a solid local bank, not too innovative, catering mainly for families. This will probably have been achieved by focus group market research. To reach its desired goal of 10 per cent market share, the bank will need to adjust this current perception of the Yuppies without alienating that held by families. So there is a quantitative target [6 per cent increase in market segment share], and a qualitative target [a more lively image]. Any future campaign of how this could be done, taking into account the positioning and perceptions of competitors, together with how the bank could become more appealing to existing and prospective customers, would need to be carefully thought through.

Chapters 3 and 6, covering alternative positioning strategies, and segmentation trends, are particularly relevant.

STEP 3: Take Action To Get There—Making it Happen

The actions you need to take to better your position may be small or large, simple or difficult. However, what must be remembered here is that people's perceptions change relatively slowly over time. So whatever actions you take will need to be repeated until the message gets through and stays put. The what and how of communications therefore is of extreme importance. In Chapter 7 we see how crucial this is when we look at how to develop positioning statements, how to create key messages for different target audiences, and how to select the most appropriate communications tools.

STEP 4: Decide Whether You Have Made It—Assessing Results

The end result of the strategic positioning pocess should be the achievement of your desired image, but this has to be checked out. We have to carry out some form of research to find out if people see things differently or just the same—more positively or perhaps more negatively. We have to find out what thoughts are in their minds that concern us. There are different ways of going about this step and they are fully discussed in Chapter 8. Perceptual mapping as a perception management and measurement technique is covered in depth, because it is not only capable of showing us where we stand in relation to our competitors, it can also reveal strategic opportunities as to which direction we should head.

FIGURE 2.2
Positioning and Image: The Virtuous Circle

Strong Position

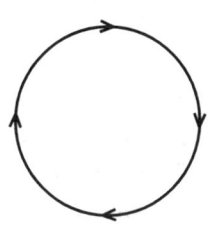

Good Image

A Virtuous Circle

Figure 2.2 shows that positioning and image go together. If you establish a good position you will enjoy a good image, and if you live up to your image you will strengthen your position. When you occupy a good position it means that you are clearly and positively differentiated from your competitors. Your image is better than theirs. If you can maintain this image and stay ahead of competitors, this consolidates your leadership position in their minds.

THE BENEFITS AND REWARDS OF STRATEGIC POSITIONING

Strategic positioning can bring enormous rewards. For a person it can mean a whole new way of looking at life positively. For struggling actors, singers, and other entertainers it can mean a rags-to-riches story. Nations are transforming global perceptions of their countries from old-fashioned to modern, low-tech to hi-tech, unattractive to attractive. In some cases, as with Taiwan, the positioning has been carried out with such force that it has been a major reason the country has to a large extent escaped the great Asian recession. Places are also benefiting. Glasgow used to be the slum of Britain, the home of thugs and gangsters, but now it is perceived as a contemporary city with a fast growing reputation for tourism. Commodity products can become valuable brands like Marlboro, credit cards can be transformed into sought after prestige luxury accessories, and companies can overcome major image problems as the company manufacturing Tylenol did, when expert public relations overcame a poisoning scare. Many such examples are scattered throughout the book, and you will also find that strategic positioning adds massive impact to the bottom line. Famous brands owe their success to strategic positioning. As illustrated in Chapter 5, not only do the top brands earn two to three times the margins of the number two competitors, but they also accrue huge equity which can be quantified in monetary terms and used to boost balance sheets and acquisition prices. Qualitatively, strategic positioning can bring to companies what they have always craved for—a magnetic attraction resulting in higher rates of customer acquisition, and unswerving customer loyalty.

To summarize, strategic positioning

1 Provides focus in what you are trying to be, and how you want to be seen.
2 Helps develop relevant messages for chosen different target audiences.
3 Tells people why you are different, why you are better, or both (in other words, explains your competitive advantage).
4 Allows you to manage people's perceptions, as opposed to relying on hope and *ad hoc* attempts to influence them.
5 Builds strong resilient reputations and images.
6 Brings sustainable wealth and success.

These are *powerful* reasons why you should read on. Plus one more. This book will show you how to do it. Although it concentrates on positioning examples intended mainly for companies and their products and services, like any strategic marketing techniques the principles are acceptable and applicable globally. Whether you wish to address your own image, that of other people, or any situation you find yourself confronted with, where there is a need to change the views and thinking of people, you will find that strategic positioning will be of enormous help. It is a necessary part of everyone's life skills.

Positioning Strategies

Thirteen Positioning Strategies

It has already been mentioned that whatever image you want to create, or however you want to influence people's minds, it has to be done strategically. In other words, positioning is a strategic and not a tactical process. Within this broad statement, however, there is much room for manoeuvre, and many approaches can be taken, which are now discussed in some detail. There are thirteen basic strategies that you can use to establish powerful positions. These strategies—and their various combinations—are described below, together with the advantages and disadvantages of using them in different situations.

1 FEATURES AND ATTRIBUTES

This is probably the most obvious one and traditionally the most frequently used in most industries. With this strategy the focus is on those characteristics of the person, company, product, place, and so on, which can be used to communicate something that is different, or better, or both.

Service companies can use this strategy, an example being the Ritz-Carlton hotel group in Asia advertising its uncompromisingly high standards. The motor vehicle industry is

FIGURE 3.1
The Thirteen Positioning Strategies

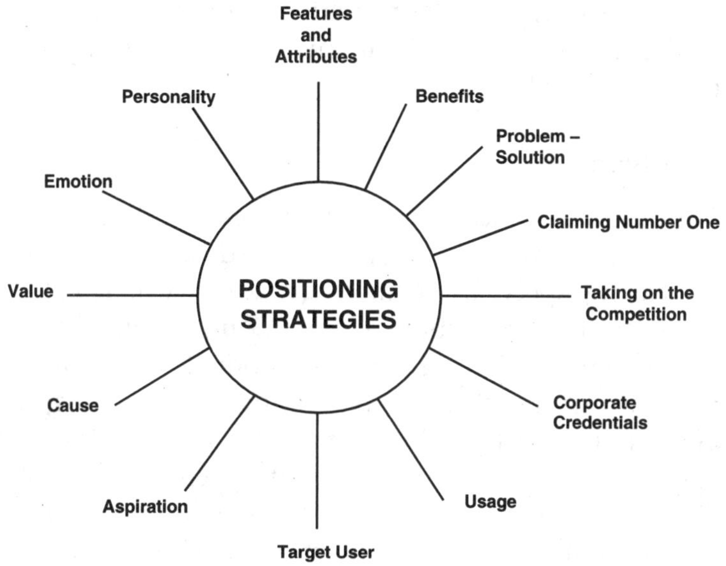

also a typical user of this strategy, and most car manufacturers either do this now or have had to do this to stay in the forefront of people's minds. Volvo for many years positioned its vehicles as being the safest on the road. Indeed, few would argue with the fact that Volvo virtually owns the characteristic of 'safety' in people's minds, despite the fact that many other cars now have similar safety features. As an example from the world of entertainment, *Baywatch* is unbelievably successful as a TV series (which claims to have over 1 billion viewers each week), based on unrivalled features that are extremely well positioned—beautiful people on beautiful beaches with apparently non-stop job excitement and satisfaction. Such positioning produces a variety of emotions in viewers.

Advantages

One advantage of this strategy is that the feature or attribute can be 'owned' for a long time as with the case of Volvo. Conversely, the association of the company with the feature might last only for a short period of time, as in the case of laser jet printers, or nasal dilatory strips. In either case, it can help create rapid market share, particularly if your product is the first in the market with a new distinctive feature or attribute. If you frequently introduce new features, then a reputation for innovation and leadership can be built. 3M, for example, is especially known for innovation, and requires that 25 per cent of sales be derived from products introduced in the last five years. Companies gain powerful positions by living their values.

Disadvantages

Truly unique features and attributes are difficult to secure these days, and they can be copied sooner or later (with increasing speed as technology advances), leading to the erosion of market-share gains. Competitors may produce enhancements that render your products obsolete, so repositioning may be difficult. Technological change is militating against this strategy due to the speed with which products can be copied, thus reducing life cycles, (more of this in Chapter 6). Finally, the strong 'ownership' of a feature can, if it is desirable to change position, become somewhat of a millstone around the company's neck. For example, Volvo has found it difficult to shift to a position based more on performance because in the minds of car buyers 'safety' is associated with heavier, not so sporty vehicles. In entertainment, stereotyping can also be difficult to break away from. The bimbo perception, for instance, makes it almost impossible for an actress labelled as such to move on to get serious roles on stage, film, or television.

2 BENEFITS

This strategy takes features and attributes to the next stage by describing what benefit(s) the customer will receive as a result. For example, a toothpaste containing fluoride (feature) helps fight decay (benefit). As competitors retaliate, more benefits are addressed, and toothpastes, like Colgate-Palmolive's Total now claim to help protect teeth against cavities, tartar, plaque, gum problems, and bad breath.

The benefits positioning strategy answers the question consumers often have in their minds: 'What is in it for me?' The safety feature of a car means protection. The introduction of airbags into cars as an additional feature might mean more expense, but in the consumer's mind the benefits of a life-saving attribute outweighs the cost.

This positioning strategy is also used by Microsoft and other companies, the features or attributes of their products leading to the articulated benefit of 'ease of use'. Telebanking and 'virtual' banking kiosks are also examples of the convenience benefit. It relies on the premise that the demand for many products and services is derived from desired benefits.

Advantages

This strategy helps give a company and its products more appeal by allowing people to see clearly what the features actually mean. Like features positioning, benefit positioning can establish short-term competitive advantage, and can lead to market leadership and quick gains. It is a reasonably flexible strategy, and can be extended either in a clinical, logical way (aimed at the left brain) or in a more emotional way (aimed at the right brain).

Example

Feature	Rational	Emotional
Safety	Protection	For your family

Disadvantage

As with the features strategy, it can be somewhat short-lived, and what is a benefit and competitive advantage today is part of tomorrow's basic product. It is based around the concept of a USP (unique selling proposition) which is vulnerable in these days to easy replication, further enhancements, and technological innovations. For instance, you may buy a personal computer with a processing speed of 'X'Mhz, currently state of the art, only to find six months later or less that 'Y'Mhz is the new industry standard for that product category.

3 PROBLEM-SOLUTION

This is another widely used and often highly effective positioning strategy. It is based on the knowledge that consumers do not necessarily want a product or service per se, but a solution to a problem they have which they think the product or company will provide. For example, people often regard some banking products as a necessary evil. It is highly unlikely they will make up in a morning gleefully shouting, 'What a great day for an overdraft!' More likely they will wake up at 3 or 4 o'clock in the morning worrying about how they are going to solve an immediate financial problem to which an overdraft might be the solution.

Similarly, slimming products offer a solution to the weight problem, and nicotine patches to the smoking problem. They are attractively positioned because people need help with personal problems that they feel are not totally within their control and might damage their health. Businesses also have many problems that they feel require outside assistance. IBM, for instance, has completely repositioned itself over the last few years by using this strategy of helping solve the problems of others. Following losses of up to US$6 billion around 1992, the company moved its positioning away from the features of its company and products to the problem–solution strategy with an advertising tag line of 'Solutions for a small planet'. It recognized that for most users, particularly corporates who were a large part of its customer-base, technology was required to solve information technology problems. The strategy has been highly successful for IBM in a marketing sense, fuelling the growth of a huge consultancy business for the company. Another giant, ABB, is also using this strategy to differentiate itself from competitors. In its advertisements, examples of problems it has solved, such as creating a new power management system in California to deal with the problems arising from deregulation and giving consumers the ability to use a power company of their choice, are highlighted with the end tag line of 'Ingenuity at Work'.

Other technology companies also adopt this approach, including British Telecom (BT), Telekom Malaysia, and Oracle. They have all realized that their customers see them as providers of solutions to communications problems. These and other companies have successfully positioned themselves combining this and other strategies.

Advantages

This strategy is clearly appropriate for certain industries such as financial services, information technology, and communications, but it is also widely applicable. Problems have always had an emotional consequence or impact on the consumer, so this is a useful strategy in that it builds in the emotion of perceived benefits. Solving people's problems also helps companies to develop trusting relationships with consumers.

Example

	Problem	**Emotional Benefit**
Life insurance	Money for family if a disaster occurs	Peace of mind for the breadwinner

Disadvantages

Other competitors can also solve the same problems consumers have, perhaps even improving on the solution. This strategy, therefore, may need reinforcement from others. For instance, people might appreciate logically that the solution is there but they need persuasion to buy, through the use of emotion.

On the other hand, it might be best to highlight a product's features to tip the balance, to help justify objectively the emotional decision, or to employ a value for money strategy, if the problem–solution is price sensitive. In technology-led industries this strategy is now becoming so overused that additional means of differentiation have to be found.

The big crunch can come if you claim the solution approach but do not deliver, as in the case of warranties that are not lived up to. Similarly, to maintain brand credibility with this strategy (particularly in technology-driven industries) new product development is vital because life cycle compression means the rapidity of new product innovations make today's problems disappear fast. The pace of change also brings to people different problems. You have to stay on top of the game here.

4 CLAIMING NUMBER ONE

If you can justify this positioning strategy for your product, service, or company, it can be a permanent source of value in developing and maintaining your brand's relationship with the consumer. Not many companies can claim to be number one, but when they are first into the market, particularly in the introduction of a revolutionary new product, they are seldom forgotten. Everyone associates Sony with the Walkman, for example, even though there are now many other brands of high quality. This is the best source of number one status as it is credible and believable. What is less effective is claiming your brand is number one on the basis of some market statistics, which mean little to the ordinary person on the street. This runs the danger of a competitor replying with a similar claim based on different statistics.

Another example of this number one or leadership positioning strategy is Charles Schwab, a company that has established itself as the number one asset manager dealing on the Internet. Other companies such as E-trade are having a hard time trying to establish their own brand names when Schwab has such a grip on the market. More than 2 million customers buy and sell stocks on the company's Internet site. Schwab does over 60 per cent of its business on-line already, with an average of 150,000 electronic transactions processed each day.

Advantage

You are widely regarded as the market leader. If you can maintain constant innovation, you will own this position.

Disadvantage

It is difficult to maintain constant innovation which requires considerable research and development investment.

5 TAKING ON THE COMPETITION

Every company has always to be aware of the competition—what it is doing and what it intends to do. Depending on competitor strategies, it may be necessary to change your position. This would be reactive strategy. On the other hand, it is possible to be proactive and change your position and thus disadvantage the competition. Writers on marketing warfare suggest that all positioning should be competitor-oriented. This, of course, is true as no company would blindly adopt a positioning strategy without reference to competitors. Marketing warfare with respect to positioning uses a military analogy to create four types of strategy.

i *Defensive Strategy*, which is for market leaders. It aims to strengthen the existing position, and block those of opponents who try to come close.
ii *Offensive Strategy*, which is for major players in, say second or third position in the market. It aims to attack the market leader's weak points.
iii *Flanking Strategy* avoids direct confrontation with market leaders, but tries to create positions near by where it can add value to market segments with slightly different products. This can be achieved by smaller players with one product, or large players with two or more products.
iv *Guerrilla Strategy*, which suits small players who want to pick off market segments that are really too small for the big fish, but can none the less be profitable. They would look for customer needs not satisfied by the bigger companies.

Advantages

Competitive strategies tend to be better for positioning companies rather than products. Corporations tend to have more unique characteristics in the form of personality, culture, size, and visual identity that people can more readily associate with, and an image that can help keep a company one step ahead when managed well.

However, in the case of products there is often less to work with in terms of 'differentiators', especially in today's increasingly cluttered markets. Notwithstanding this fact, if based on verified statistics it is possible to own a position, as demonstrated for instance, in the case of taste tests.

Disadvantages

Competitive positioning can invite retaliation, and in some countries legislation prevents it. It can lead to a lot of wasteful expenditure and embarrassing public incidents as in the case of ambush marketing. For example, it is well known that some major companies deliberately try to disrupt marketing activities such as promotional events by invading the area with their own. The message here is that you had better be sure your product or company has something to offer, which others have not, to your target audience.

6 CORPORATE CREDENTIALS OR REPUTATION

Some companies rely on the strength of the corporate name to endorse products, positioning them by the house brand reputation. This can be a very successful strategy, as demonstrated by companies such as Sony, Canon, and Nestlé. The sheer power and ubiquity of the parent company name can make life very difficult for would-be competitors trying to establish their own position. World brands such as these have for decades poured investment into creating almost invincible images that can take them around the world and into any markets they choose to enter. In other words they adopt strategic positioning principles and the resultant image strength acts as a barrier to entry of other brands into the minds of consumers.

Advantages

The power of the corporate name can help strengthen or make a strong position for even an average product. Coca-Cola's newer products are nothing startling but the magic name ensures massive sales. A well-known name can cross different markets and in some cases create global product positions, as in the case of Sony moving into the entertainment industry from consumer electronics. Alfred Dunhill has successfully moved out of cigarettes into luxury apparel and accessories.

Disadvantages

This positioning strategy relies on the company being trusted and liked above all else. If the company has a bad time so does the product, and the position can lose its credibility. A badly managed corporate image will make life very difficult for products positioned around the strength of the parental names and reputation. This was the case with Midland Bank, and was a major cause of its acquisition. Positioning was not powerful enough, promises were not delivered, and the decaying corporate image did not help new product introductions, some of which failed to reach their targets.

7 USAGE: OCCASION, TIME, AND APPLICATION

This strategy can act as an effective differentiator, although it is more appropriate for products and services than for companies and larger institutions. The strategy gains its value from the fact that people not only use products in different ways, but may do so on different occasions and at different times. For instance
- Kit Kat is eaten by some people as a snack (time usage);
- a nutritious drink like Horlicks is used by some before going to sleep (time usage) and by others as a food supplement at various times of the day (application usage);
- champagne is drunk usually only for celebrations (occasion usage).
- Maggi noodles is handy for persons in a rush and have no time to cook a full meal as it can be served in two minutes (time and occasion usage).

With positioning consistency, ownership can be total, and difficult to attack.

Advantages

Products and services can gain a market position that is more easily defendable, and the strategy is as flexible as the capability of the product's possibilities for different usage situations. Strategic positioning via this route can make for habitual usage, and thus brand loyalty. So multi-positioning is an option here (the 'one brand–many faces' issue is discussed further in Chapter 5). An example is the nasal dilatory plaster, which eases breathing difficulties offering assistance for insomniacs, snorers, sinus sufferers, and sports persons. The proposition remains the same but the positioning differs with respect to the target audience.

Disadvantages

One potential problem with the usage/occasion strategy is that your product may prove to be less effective than a competitor's product, and if the competitor can produce evidence of this, it may seize the opportunity to inform consumers and take over your position. Another area of difficulty is the fact that consumer behaviour changes over time, and consequently the time or nature of usage might change. For example, many people who have previously bought prescription and over-the-counter sinus and breathing assistance products are now wishing to be less drug dependent, and are buying externally applied products free of all possible side-effects. So the real issue with this strategy is whether or not it is sustainable for your particular situation. It demands constant market vigilance, quality leadership, and a commitment to innovation.

8 TARGET USER

The target user positioning strategy is a very good example of focus in marketing, where companies choose and get to know their target audiences well. It can be particularly effective in positioning a generic product to many customer groups, as with the case of Nike, who basically have the 'trainer' footwear dedicated to each relevant sports group. Proton cars, and other car ranges, also create variations of the product for different segments. In paints, Dulux positions its product to the do-it-yourself crowd whereas Berger positions its own to the professionals. Natwest Bank some years ago developed a small business loan for professionals such as doctors, dentists, architects, lawyers, and others and packaged it in their language with examples specific to their work. Each of these cases was successful because all the user groups *thought* (remember perception can be fact or fiction) the product had been carefully developed especially for them.

Advantages

This strategy is good for getting into niche markets and defending them, and for building strong customer relationships. Relationships with customers improve because they are being offered products that are tailored specifically to their requirements, and they feel that the company really understands and cares about what they want. It is clearly a winner for the company too. If it can develop a generic product like a training shoe, with insubstantial modifications for a wide range of customer groups to cater for slightly differing needs or applications in the form of many different sports, it allows the company to enjoy the economies of scale, and produce a wide, low-cost product range.

Disadvantages

It relies on accurate segmentation, and therefore research. Companies that do not understand the customers' real needs and wants may well come unstuck. It can be limiting, and user profiles will change over time. Nike, for instance, found it relatively easy to go from trainers to sports apparel but less easy to shift to leisure apparel. While the company had continued to attract the younger, active age group and so expand its customer base, it neglected its existing and ageing customer base, and did not position itself in the right way to accommodate their thoughts and behaviours.

9 ASPIRATION

This is a strategy that is gaining more and more favour as the world in every sense becomes more competitive. Aspirational positioning can be applied in many forms but the two common ones are concerned with
- Status and prestige (related to wealth achievement); and
- Self-improvement (related to non-monetary achievement).

In both cases the strategy relies on self-expression. Most individuals have a need to express themselves one way or another, and associating themselves with companies or brands that facilitate this is helpful.

With respect to status and prestige Rolex, Rolls Royce, and Mercedes Benz are power brands that make a statement, among other things, about their customers' financial and other achievements in life. On the self-improvement side, Nike's 'Just Do It' campaign urges people to get the best out of themselves. This type of association can also be applied, for instance, by parents for their children. Nestlé's Milo gives parents the association of wanting their children to grow up strong and healthy, and be winners.

Advantages

Aspirational positioning is inextricably linked with emotion which, when projected well, is a very successful strategy. There is a lot to be gained by appealing to the heart as well as the head, as positive emotional arousal can speed up the buying decision-making process. The aspirational positioning strategy also gains effectiveness by appealing to the self-image or desired self-image of the customer. People always have hopes and dreams of what they want to be, and whom they want to be like, and providing them with products that help them feel closer to these ideals is a powerful motivational force. This is the reasoning behind many of the extremely expensive sports personality sponsorships such as Michael Jordan and Tiger Woods. People want to be like their heroes, and will rush to buy products endorsed by them. The Jordan-endorsed sports products have been so successful that they have become a major business in their own right. Aspirational positioning has rapidly created a major global brand. If targeted correctly then, the aspirational positioning strategy can have a massive psychological impact, capitalizing on the basic human trait of optimism, hopes, and dreams about the future.

Disadvantages

One of the disadvantages of the aspiration strategy is that it does not appeal to everyone. Many people do not see themselves as winners, and nor do they want to be. If they are underachievers, for example, it may be difficult for them to associate themselves with success. So a prerequisite for this strategy is a great deal of knowledge about the behaviour and motivations of your target audience. Another more obvious concern is that the strategy can be copied without too much difficulty, as it relies on an appeal to the mind as opposed to product superiority. This again underlines the need for researching the thoughts of the target audiences involved on an ongoing basis.

10 CAUSE

This positioning strategy is also linked to emotion, and focuses on the beliefs hierarchy of people, and their need to belong. Avon, Benetton, and other companies target customer groups whom they believe will subscribe to a certain philosophy or want to relate to a specific group or movement. Avon targets women and supports women's causes, for instance by conducting a survey of 30,000 women in 43 countries to discover what they feel are their greatest challenges, what is needed for personal happiness, and what things are most important in their lives. Benetton generates messages of racial and social equality. This strategy is becoming more widely used and important as it relates to freedom of thought and speech, democracy, the liberation of women, and other social trends.

Advantages

The cause-related positioning strategy can be very powerful when linked to other strategies concerning applications, target users, and emotion. Companies can generate a strong position in this way. The Body Shop is good example of a company using this strategy, for instance by claiming it will never test its product on animals (unlike some cosmetics companies), and will make every effort to protect the environment in its search for success. The cause element is protection of the environment and the animals that live in it, and the positioning also contains a degree of emotion connected to the subject. Over time, if your company consistently espouses a worthwhile cause, considerable customer loyalty and brand equity can be built up.

Disadvantages

One problem associated with the cause-related positioning strategy is that causes can go in and out of fashion, and the degree of public support can vary over time. Additionally, a particular cause, while welcomed by some, might offend others—the gay movement being one example. It is important therefore to make sure that the cause you are embracing does not alienate your customer base. Another problem, more difficult to avoid, is that while the cause is in vogue, the 'bandwagon' effect often occurs, with many companies taking up the same cause. This has the effect of reducing the uniqueness of your position. Nowadays, for example, multitudes of companies are all too ready to promise that they will do everything they can to protect the environment.

11 VALUE

Value is often related to what people pay but this strategy is not just to do with price. There are two main elements of value positioning:

i *Price/Quality*. This means value for money, a positioning used by Marks & Spencer, No Frills, Virgin, Ikea, and Carrefour. Ikea, for example, minimizes in-store service to keep down prices, and also designs low-cost, good quality ready-to-assemble furniture and household items. In addition, Ikea gives customers added value through decorated display rooms, a cafeteria, long opening hours, and child facilities.

ii *Emotional Value*. This is the association people have when they own, for example, a Volkswagen Beetle. Volkswagen is trying to bring back these memories and emotions with an enhanced new Beetle car.

Companies can also combine the two. McDonald's has done this by successfully offering people a certain standard of quality food, at low cost, with fun for the family and kids.

Advantages

This strategy often combines the two elements, and because both elements appeal to the majority of consumers it can be used in a variety of situations. Few consumers can resist a value for money proposition, especially if backed up by emotional appeal. It also lends itself very easily for use tactically in promotions. The value strategy is also effective in targeting lower income groups, and as a market penetration strategy in emerging markets or economies, where value is a mind-set in itself and cheap is synonymous with value for money.

Disadvantages

The value strategy tends to be commodity-oriented. In other words, it is more suitable for low cost, undifferentiated products, and requires a combination of low price but reasonably good quality. It will only be successful if the company can maintain a high volume–low cost situation. It is not suitable, therefore, for those building a power brand based on prestige or status. Positioning on price/quality alone makes it very difficult to develop a prestigious image unless the powerful emotional associations can be built in. Without this element it is difficult to move into a high-perceived value/high margin situation.

12 EMOTION

As a positioning strategy this can exist on its own, but it is often used as an overlay position, adding value and strength to other strategies. It is highly important because as research shows time and time again, emotion sells. For example, Häagen-Dazs ice-cream is positioned around the concept of sheer luxury and the enjoyment of the moment. Some of the advertisements portray this with romantic and sexual imagery, and fantasy, and the success has been phenomenal. The company broke into a market dominated by giants such as Nestlé, Mars, Unilever, and others, and sold its products at up to 40 per cent higher than the others did. It was all accomplished through the creation of a unique emotionally based positioning aimed at carefully selected market segments and, more importantly, supported by consistent, appropriate advertising, promotion, and distribution.

There is nothing quite like an appeal to the heart. Johnson and Johnson baby products are positioned on 'gentleness' and 'care'—what mother can resist that sort of message? In some Asian countries the company has won 70–80 per cent market share for its products. Have you ever thought why politicians kiss the sometimes not too appealing faces of babies, and are given occasionally to weeping in front of the media? Think about the power of emotion. An appeal to the heart can overturn logic and rational analysis. Combining rational arguments and emotional positioning can be very rewarding.

Advantages

Emotional positioning strategies move people to want things. Emotion creates desire, and when coupled with rational-type strategies (see p. 49) it can be very powerful indeed. Positioning without emotion tends to be less persuasive and motivating. Positioning a can of soup merely as a soup dish appeals as a rational choice for a first course. But positioning it as highly nutritional food in its own right which will warm up and give your child a quick, healthy meal on a cold winter's day, adds the emotional touch and creates the urge to buy.

Disadvantages

As a strategy on its own, emotion might not sway the minds of the 'cold fish'—the more calculating, careful planning, thrifty types of people. For some customers price will be the decisive factor, overpowering the emotional feelings. So luxury goods will not get the same enthusiastic response with low-income groups however much emotion you inject. This again underlines the need to really understand exactly who the target audience is, and its buying behaviour. Conversely, where emotion is of use, too much of it can make consumers perceive the product unfavourably.

13 PERSONALITY

Positioning based on personality can be extremely effective, being frequently used by companies to build world class brands. (This is covered in more detail in Chapter 5). The idea behind this strategy is to build into a product or company some personality characteristics which can be projected as part of its identity, and which the target audience will find attractive. It is based on the fact that people buy things, or want to be associated with things, for what they are as well as what they do. Best practice marketing seeks to achieve the best match between what the company offers and what consumers want and need, and this offers a good opportunity to close the gap. Moreover, as far as positioning is concerned, one of the ingredients necessary for success is to ensure that the audience perceives the identity in a very positive way. People will not respond to a position they see as being either not relevant or not likeable. In either case, the perceived personality can make the difference between success and failure in both cases.

Personality characteristics such as:
- Caring
- Modern
- Innovative
- Warm
- Independent
- Strong
- Honest
- Experienced
- Genuine
- Sophisticated
- Successful

and many others have been used by marketeers to build powerful positions for products, services, companies, and people. To illustrate the power of positioning through personality, the lists below illustrate how two actual competing companies are perceived by consumers in their market.

Company A	Company B
Sophisticated	Easy-going
Assertive	Modest
Efficient	Friendly
Self-centred	Caring
Aloof	Approachable

Ask yourself the question 'Which would you prefer to have as a friend?' Around 95 per cent of people asked replied 'Company B', so it is not surprising that B is winning the battle for market share and customer loyalty. Personality positioning works because people like people, and tend to make mental judgements using personality-type words. A personality strategy can project, through advertising or other means, certain personality characteristics. As consumers perceive these, they will begin to form friendships and be loyal customers.

Advantages

People are very responsive to the personality strategy, and when combined with others it can produce high market share, loyalty, and profitability. It is a powerful way to gain and sustain a strategic competitive advantage. Concentrating your company or product positioning on personality adds strength to that personality by relating it to your competitive advantage. It tells people about your uniqueness and distinguishes you from others in a motivating way, giving them strong reasons to want to be associated with you. It is particularly useful for products that are highly visible and are more obviously 'owned' by the consumer.

Disadvantages

Personality positioning relies on a very clear understanding of the target audience, and a great deal of investment may be needed to ensure that the customer experiences a consistent personality on all occasions. Building a corporate personality, for instance, demands that the entire culture of the organization be changed so that all staff 'live' that personality in their everyday work. Building a product personality demands consistency and appropriateness in every marketing activity in order to stay true to the character created. Personality positioning is a long-term strategy.

GAINING POWER FROM COMBINING POSITIONING STRATEGIES

The positioning strategies available provide many choices. Some organizations decide to single-mindedly pursue one strategy in their efforts to change or manage consumer perceptions, as IBM does with its problem–solution choice. There is nothing wrong with sticking to one strategy, especially if competitors have not used it and it appeals to your customer base. However, some prefer to use a combination of strategies that they believe will give them a greater chance of success.

Positioning strategies can be combined in various ways to maximize persuasive appeal. An example of this is from the sports shoe and apparel manufacturer Nike, one of the world's most admired brands. *Features and attributes* are used, along with the *benefits* of improved performance, and linked to the *aspiration* of becoming a top athlete. These are all combined with *emotion* in advertisements and tag lines aimed at various *target user* groups. Similarly, in a massive advertising campaign with the caption 'Calling planet earth', Motorola tells of its new product Iridium, with a global network of sixty-six satellites (*features/attributes*) which guarantees that you can keep in touch (*emotion*) anywhere, anytime (*benefit*). The product is also positioned as being the first of its kind (*claiming number one*), which adds force to the strategies used.

Capturing Hearts and Minds with Strategic Positioning

Whatever strategies are used, the key to strategic positioning is capturing people's hearts and minds, appealing to both the rational and emotional aspects of their psychological make-up. We are all born equipped with two sides of the brain, which function in different ways. The left brain is concerned with logic, rationality, numeracy, and others while the right brain is concerned with creativity, intuition, dreams, the senses, and emotions. There are two important things about this situation which have implications for positioning. First, the two sides do not tend to work together at the same time. Secondly, you need to get the attention of both sides if you are to truly move hearts and minds. Strategic positioning then can be derived from appealing to both sides of the brain.

In consumer decisions to buy, the emotional desire is often there but the left brain requires a good logical reason to buy now, especially with luxury items. Alternatively, people sometimes accept the logic of features and benefits but need the emotional push to move them into action. Astute marketeers understand this, and combine strategies that satisfy the emotional as well as rational needs of consumers. Some companies specifically appeal to the two sides of the brain in their advertisements. Chrysler, in promoting its new Neon California model in Thailand, showed a picture of the car in the centre of the print advertisement, with consumer benefits on both sides labelled and described in detail. On the side labelled 'For your left brain' the benefits of the price, maintenance, warranty, deposit and payment structure, nationwide service network and Chrysler commitment are detailed. On the side labelled 'For your right brain', other features concerning engine size, horsepower, acceleration, safety, and country of manufacture are referred to, but with emotional phraseology such as 'Power to thrill', 'Race with the wind', 'Peace of mind', and 'Fun-to drive'. Appealing to the rational and the emotional captures both the minds and the hearts of people and hits the bottom line. Other examples of how these different needs are catered for in advertising and promotion are given in Chapter 6.

POINTS TO REMEMBER WHEN CHOOSING A POSITIONING STRATEGY

Whatever strategy or combination of strategies you eventually choose, there are certain points to be remembered:
1 The position must be salient or important to the target audience you are trying to reach and influence. It is no good communicating messages to them that are of no interest, as they will either ignore them or forget them quickly.
2 The position must be based on real strengths. Making claims that cannot be substantiated can cause enormous loss of credibility. For instance, if Johnson's Baby Shampoo caused babies having their hair washed to cry when foam touched their eyes, the positioning line claiming 'no more tears' would do endless damage to product sales.
3 The position has to reflect some form of competitive advantage. The whole point of positioning is to inform and persuade people that you are different and better than the competition, so whatever that point of difference is, it must be clearly expressed.
4 Finally, the position must be capable of being communicated simply, so that everyone gets the real message, and is motivated. The aim of positioning is to provide a call to action in the target audience, so any communication must be created with this in mind.

These points will be dealt with in a practical sense in Chapter 7.

CASE STUDY

THE CARAT CLUB: ACHIEVING DIFFERENTIATION AND REPOSITIONING THE COMPETITION

The Carat Club was set up as the retail arm of a wholesale diamond supplier to the jewellery industry in Malaysia and Singapore. Jewellery retailing in Asia tends to be characterized by lots of outlets manned by seemingly large numbers of staff behind huge long counters waiting to pounce on any customer who puts a foot through the door. It is essentially a commodity type market, with heavy bargaining and discounting. The owners and management of The Carat Club decided to change the rules, putting the customer first, and creating a new category of retailing.

The 'club' concept means that customers can come to a comfortably furnished venue with a library area where refreshments are served. (In Kuala Lumpur, the Club is set up in a bungalow located in an up-market area.) There are books and videos to look at so that customers can gain knowledge and buy with greater confidence. A cosy atmosphere is created by having several serving areas where customers can receive greater attention but maintain privacy. The whole aim is to provide an environment where the customers are not intimidated, and where education eliminates the fear of being cheated. With the knowledge customers acquire comes the appreciation of, and passion for, the mystique and incredible beauty of fine jewellery. This leads to a confident purchase and peace of mind, and what remains is the afterglow of ownership that will last a lifetime. Customers also receive a photograph of their treasured purchase, and an authenticity certificate.

The Carat Club segments its customers by life stages. In most instances, the first diamond may be purchased by a person in the mid-twenties. This is usually an engagement ring. This is then followed by purchases for birthdays, anniversaries, birth of children, and others. Industry statistics reveal that an average couple makes thirty-two jewellery purchases in their lifetime; hence it is important to capture them at first purchase, and retain their loyalty. So special product brands are created for different life stages and occasions. For example, the 'Love Diamond' is targeted at the bridal market, and has a unique cut that displays hearts and arrows within it. Other product brands created include ones such as 'Everyday Treasures' for young working professionals who are looking for that special accessory to make them feel and look good. More intricate and stunning designs are made for other market segments. Prices are also affordable as the company, through its wholesaling division, can eliminate some of the third party margins.

The Carat Club has deliberately fostered a corporate personality of being
- Trustworthy
- Friendly
- Confident
- Contemporary
- Stylish
- Innovative
- Sophisticated

The ambience, service standards, and personal touches make the personality come alive. By positioning itself in this way, and with value for money, it has differentiated itself from the competition, and now owns this new category of jewellery retailing.

Repositioning

REPOSITIONING

Most positioning is in fact repositioning, unless you have a new company or product that no one has heard of yet. If you are currently established in the market-place, even though it might not have been for a long time, you will find that people already have a view of you. An image will have already been formed in their minds. This does not mean that the strategies described in the previous chapter do not apply—they work in both circumstances. In most situations though, it is positional change that is required. There are several reasons why repositioning may be necessary, but the eight major reasons why companies attempt to reposition themselves or their products are:

- Poor or outdated image
- Fuzzy, blurred image
- Change in target audience or their needs and wants
- Change in strategic direction
- New or revitalized corporate personality/identity
- Change in competitor positioning or new competitors
- Momentous event
- Rediscovery of lost values

1 POOR OR OUTDATED IMAGE

For whatever reason, your present image may fall short of your desired consumer perception. British Rail has had a continuous struggle with its image, which was found to be difficult to alter even though privatization changed the whole nature of the organization. In the technology industry, Unisys has a new advertising campaign to replace their outdated positioning as the 'Information Management Company', because management feels that people now perceive the company as a dull old-line maker of big mainframe computers. The new positioning, intended to get people to think of the company as a services company with a technology arm, is reflected in modern offbeat advertisements portraying employees constantly thinking about their work whatever they are doing, with the tag line 'We eat, sleep and drink this stuff'. Time will tell whether this strategy will change perceptions.

Many companies around the world are now faced with debt restructuring and other problems affecting perceptions and confidence in them, but despite new management and other improved aspects, negative associations from the past linger in customers' minds. The temporary halt to the progress of the 'Asian economic miracle' has given not only many companies but also countries in the region an urgent reason to reposition themselves. Malaysia is one such country that has had a repositioning issue to deal with in the wake of the dreadful crash of currencies and business disasters which started in July 1997 and which spread rapidly to all the other Asian countries. The rest of the world's perception was interesting, because no one saw any difference between the different countries involved. They were treated exactly the same by commentators, analysts, investors, and the like. In reality, Malaysia was not in the same degree of distress as most of the others and, as time has shown, did not need to call for the International Monetary Fund (IMF) or other agencies for international financial assistance. It has a stronger economic foundation and, despite being hard hit, has not experienced the same casualty rate, as the others. Nevertheless, in people's minds, it was lumped together with the rest and is still suffering from a lack of investor confidence.

Once again we are reminded that perception is reality, and as far as Malaysia is concerned more effective repositioning strategies are needed to regain reputation, confidence, and global image.

2 FUZZY, BLURRED IMAGE

Sometimes the perception people have of your company or product is not clear. It is not that it is poor—it may be that people do not think strongly about it one way or the other. The Kent cigarette brand has had this problem of indifference in one Asian country where mental associations by consumers were weak compared to other cigarette brands. In such a case, repositioning was necessary to liven up or revitalize the brand, and to make it stand for something in people's minds. Some aggressive advertising and promotion campaigns were carried out, but the company is finding that changing consumer perceptions takes time and a lot of perseverance.

A fuzzy or blurred image usually results from an inadequate, unclear brand identity. This happens where the company has failed to project what it or its product really stands for, and how different its product is from other brands.

3 CHANGES IN TARGET AUDIENCE OR THEIR NEEDS AND WANTS

If the marketing focus changes, then repositioning is a must. Theoretically, this might prove difficult depending on whether the new focus is relatively close to or far away from the previous one. So, for instance, if Coca-Cola decided to target the over 60's age group, repositioning would not only be necessary, but a major challenge in convincing those people that the product was not a drink made for the younger set.

When considering extending the marketing of your company or product to new market segments, it is imperative that a reality check is carried out through market research to see whether a new position is feasible and whether the task would be too large and costly, perhaps even damaging the perceptions held by existing customer groups. If Coke tried to access the over 60s segment with the major advertising necessary, what would young people think and do? In the world of entertainment, one person who has made the successful move is Madonna. Madonna has successfully shifted to a different target market by singing music geared to a higher age profile, moving away from performances that appealed to youth. This has enabled her to extend her career into musicals and acting in productions like *Evita*. This is equivalent to product line extension, and Madonna has changed features and attributes to suit target audiences through dress, appearance, and frequent press interviews about motherhood responsibilities. She has adopted a more toned down public profile and positioning to extend her attraction to a wider range of audiences.

A variation of this reason for repositioning is where, although the target audience remains much the same, ages and needs of the customer base change. In this situation the company has to try to keep up with these changes (whether in thinking or behaviour) if it is going to keep the customers.

Brylcreem, in the 1950s and early 1960s, was a hair preparation that provided a greasy, flattened look for young men. It has since had to reposition the brand to become more modern and up-to-date and keep pace with men's fashions. Its existing customer base grew up with fashion-based needs such as a more full-bodied look and so on, hence gel preparations. To help in the repositioning effort, the company has used endorsements by top young personalities whom its target audience will relate to, such as Manchester United footballer David Beckham.

Nike is also in the process of adjusting its brand positioning a little as it has also found that its original customer base is getting older and feeling a little less like 'just doing it', and the youngsters are no longer identifying with it as children previously did. The new positioning still relates to self actualization as with their old tag line of ' Just Do It' but in a less aggressive and energetic way. The new slogan is 'I Can', which Nike believe will be perceived in a more positive way by all audiences. They have also been forced by consumers to defend allegations that the factories in the Third World subcontracted to make their products were exploiting labour with harsh terms and conditions of work. In this instance, a robust public relations campaign was needed to protect Nike's image. In this sort of case the company has to respond quickly to consumer expectations if it is to restore its desired image. Even the British Broadcasting Corporation (BBC) has had to listen to its customers, who have made it clear that its World Service is a little too highbrow for their liking. A major effort is now being made to present programmes which will reposition the corporation and the image of that division.

Sometimes, structural alterations in the industry or market force companies to reposition. This is the case with recent changes in the drugs/pharmaceutical industry in the United States, where the Food and Drug Administration (FDA) now allows a more relaxed form of advertising giving manufacturers the opportunity to omit lengthy disclaimers and warnings and advertise direct to the general public as opposed to doctors. The target audience has changed, and advertisers are now researching the new targets so that appropriate positioning messages can be projected. So far, they have discovered three different types of pill-takers.

i *Information Actives:* those who will take the initiative and call toll-free numbers for more information.
ii *Indifferents:* those who are basically apathetic about health matters.
iii *Passives:* those who need to be pushed or prodded to take their medicine.

The agencies developing their positioning through commercials are thus having to create different ways of appealing to these distinctive market segments.

Lucozade is another good example of strategic positioning for a different target audience. For many decades, this product was positioned as a restorative drink for the elderly and infirm, being glucose-based and consequently a source of energy for people who needed a diet supplement. More recently it has been targeted at sports enthusiasts as a quick and easy energy enhancing drink, to provide that extra bit of performance. Lucozade has achieved a good deal of success in this, breaking through into a fairly new category against already established competitors and gaining entry into a new and substantial market. Repositioning of this sort may require a strategic change of direction.

4 CHANGE IN STRATEGIC DIRECTION

One type of directional change required is when there is a need to move from one product category to another. This situation usually arises when the category a product is in becomes too crowded, and symptoms of high competitive pressure such as the erosion of sales and margins occur. Perceptual mapping research (discussed in Chapter 8) will reveal just how close the competitors are positioned in the minds of people who buy from that category, and what spaces, if any, are available in that or other categories. These categories exist in consumer minds and should not be defined by a company—they depend on how people organize information about the things they see, whether it is by name, usage, attribute, or other descriptors. If we take an example similar to that mentioned above, a Mars chocolate bar could be seen as a mid-morning snack, an energy source for the athletically inclined, a nutritional aid for illness recovery, or simply a great sweet for children. Successful category repositioning depends on the product having the attributes necessary for acceptance by consumers in the new category, and this should be tested out prior to re-launch as slight product modifications or enhancements and repackaging may prove to be necessary. Care should be taken to ensure correct definition of perceived categories.

In some cases it may be desirable strategically to enter totally new markets or even new industries. In such a case repositioning will be necessary to assure the new markets of your credibility, as you step out of your familiar role and compete with those names with which consumers more readily associate the product.

Laura Ashley, the famous British home furnishings and clothing retail chain, has failed to keep up with the times and cast off its traditional image. As a consequence it has become the subject of merger/acquisition activity, with Malayan United Industries ending up the winner. Clearly a repositioning strategy is needed. The name of the company conjures up a vision of old England and old-fashioned flowery products (which for many years was a very successful position with female audiences), and that image still lives on. The problem in this case is that fashion trends have changed and although the style and quality of Laura Ashley products still commands respect, they no longer command sales.

There is, however, a lot of brand equity left in the name, and here is a case where adjustments to product ranges and outlets have to be made, and where the brand itself needs repositioning to capture a wider customer base. Any proposed investment needs to revitalize and reposition the famous name, building on the strengths it has acquired over the years. Laura Ashley needs to go through the whole power positioning process. The issue is to link identity (which it has) with modernity (which it has not).

5 NEW OR REVITALIZED CORPORATE PERSONALITY/IDENTITY

This is the corporate equivalent of plastic surgery. Some companies find it worthwhile to completely change their identity—not just with a new logo—but possibly with a name change, a new structure, and a new personality, in order to overcome problems of the past, or to take advantage of new opportunities. The name change from Lucky Goldstar to LG is a recent example, as the company attempted quite successfully to move upmarket with its image, and target more profitable customer groups.

In Asia today there are many companies that have local perceptions that do not match international aspirations. Well-known, Chinese-named (and often family-owned) companies, for instance, have the challenge of moving away from current perceptions and projecting a more corporate, professional image.

Tag Heuer, the well-known sports watchmaker, has used an expensive global advertising campaign involving eleven sports personalities in an effort to move away from the current cold, mechanical, technically efficient image to one which is perceived as warmer and more human. The basic position of mental attitude overcoming adversity and being in control of oneself is still present. However, the company says 'through the association of the brand with these key players in sports, who have succeeded through sheer physical and mental effort, we hope to make a comeback to a more humane face'.

Sometimes companies have to revitalize well-known brands that have been around for a long time, and position them as being more modern and 'with it'. Chanel, a brand that is well over seventy years old, is one case in point. Categories like fashion are very susceptible to changing perceptions of consumers, and have to keep themselves fresh and young. Chanel, like other big brand companies, uses advertising campaigns to achieve this, and in one recent campaign introduced fantasy into its commercials based on the fairy-tale of Little Red Riding Hood, adding sophistication and sex as per the industry norm. The result was a repositioning that revitalized the Chanel identity, and appealed to younger audiences as well as its traditional customer base. The promotion was on MTV as well as in the more upmarket magazines in print advertisements that maintained the classic aspects of the brand but with added modernity.

6 CHANGE IN COMPETITOR POSITIONING

Sometimes the competition moves closer to your own positioning, and you may feel it is best to move away by repositioning. BMW in the United States had to do this when Lexus encroached upon its position and started to erode its customer base. Bentley faced a similar problem. Though owned and produced by the same company, Bentley cars were perceived for many decades as the cheaper version of the Rolls Royce cars. This was thought to be a position that endangered sales of both vehicles, particularly of Bentley. The repositioning of Bentley cars, through the creation of a more sporty image supported by product development with high performance engines, moved it away from the 'poor relation' perception into a powerful position as the world's most luxurious sports vehicle. Sales soared and it has become one of the most successful repositioning stories.

7 MOMENTOUS EVENT

Occasionally a traumatic event might occur which demands repositioning. Privatization is one example affecting many organizations in Asian countries. Utility companies, for instance, are often in need of repositioning to change people's attitudes towards, what was, a government entity, with a perceived government bureaucracy mind-set. An alternative momentous event could be a sudden, unexpected crisis, such as the poisoning incidents faced by Tylenol and Perrier. Momentous events can be good or bad, and can affect not just companies but individuals and nations too. Michael Jackson, Madonna, and Mike Tyson have all had image crises in recent years, and Pepsi at one stage had endorsement deals with each of them—an unfortunate *coup* at the time. Most South-east Asian countries have suffered from a poor image and a consequent lack of investor confidence due to the economic crisis, and thus need to work hard at repositioning themselves.

8 REDISCOVERING LOST VALUES

Sometimes when a brand has reached a point where consumers are almost taking it for granted, a company may feel that instead of trying to create an entirely new position, it might be worthwhile going back and looking at the successful strategies of the past, or using the past. Kellog's once ran a campaign for Corn Flakes with the tag line 'Try Them Again For The First Time'. Such a strategy based on brand heritage can be very successful especially when competitors are relatively new and the target audiences are open to the emotional value of nostalgia. It can easily answer in their minds the questions of why that company or product is different and better. R.H.M.'s Hovis bread also ran a great campaign featuring its products, which had been available for many decades, presented in an old world (north of England) setting, representing the old days and the values of a nation fighting through hard work to develop itself. Nostalgia is an underestimated positioning vehicle. Used judiciously, it gives people a reason to get involved.

Another example of going back is where there has been a departure over time from the core values of a company, product, or person. The successful repositioning of the Asda superstore chain, based in Yorkshire, was based on recognition of the fact that it had moved away from its original values and its unique positioning as a company from which you could buy nearly everything at lowest cost. This was the strategic platform upon which it had built one of Britain's most profitable and fastest growing businesses. But it forgot the golden rule of remaining true to its position and started to try to beat the competition by appealing to different customer groups with a different value proposition, and ended up losing its way, its customers and its profits. It took around five years of hard work, self-analysis, and sheer determination in rediscovering its values, and repositioning, not to mention having the guts to run campaigns saying 'We're back'. Transparency and honesty are values close to the hearts of today's consumers.

Success can change people too. How often have you heard that someone you know has changed since 'he made it', or that 'coming into money has changed her'? People like people much more when they remain as the person they trust and have known for a long time—friends who stay true to their values and personality.

REPOSITIONING THE COMPETITION

As an alternative to moving your position, would it not be a better idea to change consumer perceptions about competitors? The rationale of this strategy is to avoid being forced to be on the defensive by aggressive competitor tactics, you strengthen your own position and influence consumer preferences and perceptions to put your competitors at a disadvantage. This can be a powerful repositioning strategy, but there may be a risk of failure and damage to your image that might ensue. How this might be done needs to be taken into account. For example, how far can you go in repositioning the competition in the light of the country's advertising standards regarding what is and is not acceptable or allowable?

Nevertheless, there are some good examples of competitor repositioning. Swatch has repositioned Japanese watch brands. Swiss watchmakers lost most of their world market share to the Japanese after underestimating the impact of the quartz movement (as it happens, invented by them!); Swatch was an exception to this demise. They replied by creating a huge market for cheaper fashion watches. They spotted a gap in the market between two major watch positions—those representing *functionality* and *representationality*. The functionality positioned watches were low-cost, short-term purchase items, mainly Japanese with brands like Casio. Those in the representationality category were the high-cost, glamorous, prestige, often long-term investment buys like Piaget. Swatch successfully exploited the gap, taking market share mainly from the functional side. They did this by developing a wide range of medium-cost, limited design run watches, thus creating a 'fashion' and 'fun' category. Tag Heuer has successfully repositioned the prestige watches like Rolex with the younger high achievers in Asia through outstanding advertising campaigns that have also allowed them to significantly raise their prices and margins.

In attempting this strategy you will need to rigorously analyse the competitor(s) and look for any areas of acceptability or unreliability in their brands. Although a seemingly negative, reactive strategy, repositioning the competition is very proactive and needs aggressive advertising and promotion to succeed. It also requires a complete understanding of the needs of the target customer groups, which means ongoing market research to establish changing market circumstances and relative customer perceptions.

MULTIPLE REPOSITIONING

A related question is whether it is wise to change positions more than once, or indeed, several times. This issue is also referred to in Chapter 5, with respect to one brand having many faces, but here I will address it as a repositioning issue.

Sometimes it is necessary to change position in order to accommodate the needs of, and penetrate new market segments. This is not the same as line extension, which extends the company, person, or product name to different things offered, and possibly different consumer groups. An example here is the Spice Girls who are putting their name(s) to many different products without moving away from their basic position. Repositioning changes extend the same name to either the same or new customer groups without changing in any significant way what is on offer. This is often done to widen the customer base. This demands skill because the product is essentially the same in terms of features, attributes, and values yet somehow it has to be made to appeal to different customer groups having different needs, wants, and expectations. If the new position is too far away from the basic position or loses relevance, then there is not only the danger of not getting accepted into the new market segment, but also the real prospect of losing existing customers who no longer feel it is for them.

One of the most successful companies that have taken this challenge on is Guinness with its classic beer (stout) product. The company now has many products in its portfolios but the original black beer is a famous brand in its own right. It has had to achieve this success by changing the way in which the product is positioned to attract different segments of the population. For instance, around twenty years ago, particularly in the UK/Ireland home market, the typical customer could have been described socio-demographically as an older working-class male. Young people and women occupied a small proportion of the customer base. In the 1980s the marketing mix, including packaging, distribution channels, and advertising campaigns, were completely revamped to attract more women and people higher up the income scale without disillusioning the present customers, presenting the velvety, creamy texture of the drink in situations of upmarket social occasions. This resulted in significant increases in sales and market share in the newly targeted segments, with little attrition in the original customer base.

While the above positioning changes were meant for the home market, the 1990s challenge was to keep all existing customers again, but lower the age profile further to encompass the 18–35 age bracket. A tough assignment, but it is positioning that holds the key, and again it seems to be working for Guinness. With advertising that appeals to younger men, featuring scenes such as people ending a physically challenging activity with a pint of Guinness, and use of strong words like 'Big Pint', the company is making significant inroads into more youthful markets, including Asian markets where the average age of national populations is low, and products relatively new and unaccepted. So it is back to the core values again, and understanding different consumers, but there is little doubt that Guinness will achieve world brand status.

So positions can change as long as you do not move too far away from your true identity. If you can change positioning but basically remain who you are, celebrity status will be achieved whatever business you are in. In the world of entertainment look at the Rolling Stones, Paul McCartney, Michael Jackson, Cliff Richard, the Bee Gees, Bob Dylan, Eric Clapton, and Elton John. They have not really altered their product, but they have changed how they present themselves to appeal to new market segments through positioning techniques—they have versatility in communicating with their audiences.

REVOLUTIONARY VERSUS EVOLUTIONARY POSITIONING

REVOLUTIONARY POSITIONING

Sometimes the question is asked as to whether positioning should take place in a dramatic or a gradual way. Revolutionary positioning is a term that tends to be applied to a situation where you are starting from square one, say with a new product, company, or personal goal. In such a situation there is no current image, and a position has to be created for the first time. In other words, once you are nowhere you have to go somewhere. In this case strategic positioning has to be revolutionary. You have to choose a powerful position amidst all the established competitors and make an impact. Tommy Hilfiger is a good example of powerful, revolutionary positioning. This is a brand of clothing that broke into the fashion market for young people in the midst of intense competition and became a significant world-wide force almost overnight. The strategy illustrated the branding process well.

- Choose the target
- Give them something new, but understand what they want, whether it is a new style, a new icon, and so on
- Give it a personality and position it well
- Deliver the right key messages
- Keep the marketing communications consistent

In the world of fashion there is always room for a new personality, and personality combined with accurate positioning made this brand one of today's most desired product ranges. This was, of course, no easy task. It took a great deal of time, research, and money, but it does show that even in the most competitive of markets, strategic positioning works.

EVOLUTIONARY POSITIONING

Evolutionary positioning, on the other hand, is about developing your image and protecting it in the face of changing market circumstances. Here the issue is that once you are somewhere, you have to decide where to go next and not be left behind. This is a repositioning problem and it can be extremely dangerous. The danger lies in suddenly stepping completely away from the position you have been occupying, and to which consumers, particularly existing customers, are accustomed without alienating them and losing your unique identity. For example, Georgio Armani, in an interview with Cable News Network (CNN), described his biggest problem as how to keep his classic design styling and at the same time adopt fashionable change. He saw it as a true dichotomy. On the one hand, the existing customer base expects to see his classic style. On the other, fashion is moving faster, due to technological advances and media hype. Armani said that the media are now less sensitive to individual style and more sensitive to what mass designers are producing. So if the mass design latest fashions include the colour red, everyone (Armani included) is expected to deliver something in red. If not, he said, he would be left out of media support for that season. The dilemma for designers like Armani is therefore how to remain constant to his distinctive style, that is, *positioning*, and yet incorporate the newest of the new. His answer is evolutionary change, not revolutionary change. He has to position his products to satisfy the conflict of identity versus modernity. He must remain constant to his customers and meet their expectations both of classic style and contemporary fashion. An evolutionary tightrope so far walked successfully by one of the masters of fashion—with the help of strategic positioning.

CASE STUDIES IN REPOSITIONING

MITSUBISHI MOTORS

Mitsubishi Motors in the United States has more than one reason when in 1998 it launched a US$40 million to 50 million programme to reposition its brand. Focus group research revealed that brand awareness was very low, and consumers had no clear views on the brand. In other words, the image was weak and blurred, many people confusing it with other divisions of the parent group which is probably better known for its electronics products. As Pierre Gagnon, executive vice-president and chief operating officer of Mitsubishi Motor Sales of America, Inc. (MMSA) said, 'It's time for consumers to start associating our individual models with the image of Mitsubishi Motors and for us to stand behind that image in order to create more awareness about our brand.' One of the reasons that prompted this view was its market share which remained largely static at about 1.2 per cent. The company is seeking to increase this through better market segmentation and by targeting what it believes to be a gap in the market, in the form of a segment of people who want to look attractive, have fun, and stay young. Features of the car models, particularly the Galant, such as styling and brake horse-power, and value-for-money, low-price strategies are all included in the commercials, in a multi-strategic, single-minded attempt to provide specific customer groups with a tightly focused communication. The 'Wake up and Drive' campaign theme is especially designed to bring about a brand image which combines a balanced perception of product excellence and emotional attachment.

The 'fun-to-drive' advertisement series is apparently similar to those of companies targeting younger audiences, using MTV music and messages to project the emotional thought that everyone wants to feel young and have some excitement in their lives, whatever their age. Mike Sheldon, the executive vice-president and general manager of Deutsch Inc., Mitsubishi's ad agency, said 'We were charged with taking a product that blended quality, durability, style and fun and then creating an overall image that stirred the emotions.'

BLUE NUN

The Blue Nun wine brand from Germany is familiar to many people around the world. Traditionally, it has been positioned at the low end of the market being exported in bulk and priced inexpensively in its distinctive brown bottle with the blue-habited Nun. In the 1970s and 1980s it achieved considerable success.

However, the brand has been reformulated and relaunched. The composition of the wine has changed and it is no longer a *Liebfraumilch*, the category label associated with downmarket wines with different quality grapes. Consumer tastes have changed and cheap sweet wines are now losing their appeal, resulting in the lowering of demand and profits. The repositioning of Blue Nun has involved removing *Liebfraumilch* from its label and replacing it with *Qualitaetswein Rheinessen* reflecting its improved quality while retaining the heritage of its origin. The aim of course is to raise the image (and hence prices) and to turn the brand around. In addition to raised prices and changed contents, the new bottles are now marine blue instead of brown, but Blue Nun still remains on the label.

Other German wine producers have acted similarly with their *Liebfraumilch* products using clear bottles and simple labels, but the Blue Nun will stay as a symbol of this brand. What remains to be seen is whether or not the old mental associations of the Blue Nun (sweet cheap wine) can be changed. It will probably take a few years and lots of advertising and promotion to reposition the brand as once consumer perceptions are entrenched, they are slow and difficult to change.

SCANDINAVIAN AIRLINE SYSTEM

Changing customer tastes, preferences, and perceptions plus a highly competitive market have led the three-country consortium Scandinavian Airline System (SAS) to completely reposition itself, the idea being to capture the personality essence of the Scandinavian countries of Norway, Denmark, and Sweden (the three countries are similar in history, language, culture, and lifestyle). The main personality characteristics are:

- Simple yet effective
- Direct and honest
- Humble and not fussy
- Elegant but not pompous
- Trustworthy and reliable
- Caring
- Warm

At first sight this seems a complex list of traits, but human personalities are complex, and SAS has certainly tried hard to reflect this multi-faceted personality across all products and services

Apart from new livery, state-of-the-art technology, and caring, environmentally protective unique specifications are all designed to soothe the safety, reliability, and technical concerns that consumers have. A great deal of thought has also gone into themed innovation in other respects. Elegance in interior design is combined with simple lighting and colours. Plane, lounge, and airport interiors as well as the meals are given a domestic, more personal feel to create the emotional characteristics of warmth and hospitality or as the company puts it 'nearness'. The total cost is enough to raise eyebrows in the biggest of boardrooms, but that is what it takes to deliver on the promises offered by a new positioning for a major product.

Positioning and Branding

Branding

WHAT IS BRANDING?

Branding has been around for several hundred years. In its most traditional form it was a mark burned on to an animal or possession to show which person or group of people owned it. In this respect, branding has not changed, as companies have to somehow differentiate themselves and their products and services from those of their competitors. Branding as we know it now originated in this way, and companies use logos, symbols, names, and designs to distinguish themselves and their products and services from each other. However, branding has come a long way from being a relatively simple name or design act to a complex art, and major companies go to extreme lengths by investing time, people, and a lot of money into the branding process. Branding is a sophisticated process that can result in returns far and away beyond individual recognition.

IS BRANDING REALLY POSITIONING?

The main aim of branding is to create an individual identity for a product or service (although other things can be branded) that will make it different from all other competitive offers. It could be argued that a brand is really only a position, because without a position a brand is only a company, product, service, and so on. The reasoning behind this is that the position makes the brand because it creates the value in the minds of the target audience.

Whether this argument is totally true or not, it must be accepted that positioning is vital to brand building, because it takes the basic tangible aspects of the product and builds the intangibles, in the form of an image, in peoples' minds. It focuses on the chosen target audience(s) and influences their thoughts about the brand in relation to other brands. Through the strategies described in the previous chapter, positioning uses the best ways of convincing people that a particular product is both different and better than any other. This chapter explains how and why brands are built, and the critical role played by positioning in making the strategic leap from being perceived as an ordinary brand to being seen as world class, with all the rewards this brings. Strong or even world class branding is impossible without strategic positioning

HOW VITAL IS BRANDING?

Branding is important because when done well it probably provides the best returns on investment in the world. The financial rewards can be spectacular. For example, when Nestlé bought Rowntree they paid over five times the net asset value of the company in order to have in their stable the famous brands such as Kit Kat and Smarties, which year on year provide endless streams of profit. Ford Motor Co. paid US$2.4 billion for Jaguar and invested a further US$6 billion to modernize it. Big brands mean big money, but the rationale for branding remains the same—strong differentiation from your competitors.

There are other benefits accruing from branding also. Strong brands stand the test of time. In many industries today the leading brand names are those that occupied the same dominant position sixty to seventy years ago—Colgate and Coca-Cola for instance. Coca-Cola is well over 100 years old but it still looks young and is still growing. Brands like these also command price premiums, several times more than competitors. One study showed that people would pay over US$400 more for an IBM than for a comparable Dell or Compaq, despite identical chips and similar performance.

So what makes a strong brand? How do companies build strong brands? And why do people spend so much just to acquire them? The answers to these questions are the subject of this chapter, but first of all there is the question of what can be branded and what constitutes a brand.

CAN ANYTHING BE BRANDED?

The answer is 'Yes'. We all know of branded products like British Airways' Concorde, companies like Nestlé, and services like FedEx. But we often forget that people can be branded too, like Madonna, Tony Blair, and Elvis Presley. Tourist destinations like Singapore, and entertainment chains like Hard Rock Café are all examples of good branding. New Orleans, for instance, is branded as the 'Home of Jazz'. Anything or anyone can be branded. The degree of success depends to some extent on the quality of the product or person, but more depends on how well the branding process is carried out. Brand specialists go about the process in different ways depending on what they are branding but they tend to use one basic strategic platform.

WHAT IS A BRAND?

A normal dictionary-type description would say that a brand is an identifying name, mark or label, or a trademark used to distinguish products of particular companies. But branding is more than just creating a logo, a catchy name, a trademark or a good product, although logos and names are the visual parts of a brand that consumers look for, and can develop strong associations in peoples' minds. They could be said to be part of the features of a brand.

Although a brand is a complex mixture of elements, its composition is really made up of three things:

1 *Features.* This might be the technical specifications for a product, or the size and structure of a company.
2 *Benefits.* These are the needs and wants that the brand will satisfy for those who buy it.
3 *Values.* Values in this sense are the more intangible aspects of the brand—often the associations or feelings that people have with or about it—like prestige and status, and other things they identify with.

The key to successful brand building is the way in which the three items are combined to form a brand identity, and whether the brand image matches that identity. The features and benefits associated with a brand may not make it particularly unique. It tends to be the values customers feel a brand possesses that makes it different. Strategic positioning plays a major role in this process by defining and projecting those values in the form of a strong brand identity, and this creates the image of the brand.

Brand Identity and Brand Image

Many people refer to terms such as brand identity and brand image, and often confuse their meaning, which can lead to expensive mistakes in the world of business.

All brands must have an identity. A person's identity might be made up of the way he or she dresses, speaks, acts, moves, and whether they are reliable, honest, hard-working, and so on. A product can also be like this. It can be physically dressed differently (packaging), speak differently (through the tone of voice of advertising commercials), and have other specific characteristics such as reliability. The sum total is its identity—it is the whole of what is being offered. As with people, so with places, countries, products, services, and companies—their identity involves depth, substance, character, performance, and other factors. The aim of providing brands with identities (and names are also a part of this process) is to get people to see them as being unique in some way—to generate a particular image.

Brand image, however, may not turn out to be the same as the identity we want. Image, as mentioned in Chapter 1, is subject to perception—the way in which people think about or even imagine something to be. So if identity is projected wrongly, or not strongly enough, it might be perceived wrongly. For instance, people might not see us as honest, or might think our packaging looks cheap. Such a difference between identity and image is what is often called the 'perception gap', and this must be avoided at all costs. So when a brand is being built, great care must be taken to ensure that the image matches the identity.

HOW BRANDS ARE BUILT

To avoid the 'perception gap' between identity and image we must make sure that what we want people to see or think is perceived accurately. Not forgetting that the brand has its own features and benefits that customers will recognize, the key differentiator will almost certainly be the unique values that customers perceive it has. Building the brand on a firm strategic platform creates these values and customer perceptions of them. There are two main aspects to building a strategic brand platform and these are

- Brand Personality—which creates a unique identity; and
- Strategic Positioning—which creates the image.

FIGURE 5.1
Building a Strong Brand Platform

Brand Identity and Image

Brand Personality   **Strategic Positioning**

Brand Personality

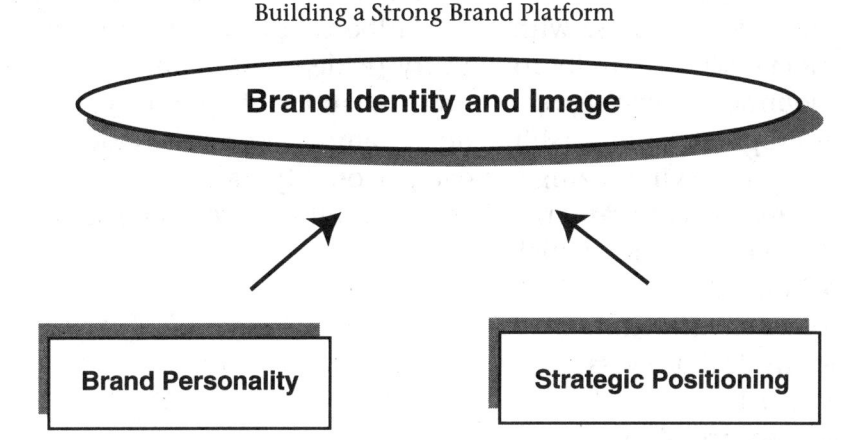

The attraction of a strong personality is irresistible, and the clever marketeers build personality into their companies, products, services, countries, and places. A good example of this is the Nestlé product Milo (known in different parts of the world by different names—a global product with local adaptations), which is a chocolate-based drink. The brand has always had, since 1934 when it was launched, the brand values of:

- Great taste
- Healthfulness and energy
- Winning moments

The target audiences are parents and, of course, their children. The personality is always presented as young people winning sports events, or achieving something demanding physical fitness and health.

The brand values of Milo are not entirely those of a 'person' as such—they are a mix of product-related and personality-related characteristics or traits, and some companies find it useful to present a mix when building the identity. What is important, however, is that they are projected properly, that is, positioned as a personality.

One of the world's most famous brands, on the other hand, has built its identity on just two personality characteristics. The brand is Marlboro and the characteristics are strength and independence. Again, nothing startling as a personality, but the projection of these characteristics has made the brand world class, with the Marlboro cowboy (strong and independent), Marlboro country (wide open plains and big mountains), packaging (strong red and white colours), and appropriate sponsorships (for example, Formula One car racing) all symbolizing the two personality traits.

Levi 501 is a brand that has been built with seven personality characteristics, which are:
- Romance
- Sexual attraction
- Physical prowess
- Rebellion
- Resourcefulness
- Independence
- Admiration (from others)

Personality is the foundation for many successful brands, and companies concentrate on this for good reasons. First, people like people—they like to be with people, have friends, and work and play with other people. They also tend to make judgements about things in personality terms. They will think and say things like 'I like that company' or 'That product is not very nice'. Also, they tend to buy brands which fit in with their own self-concept, or one to which they aspire to be; in other words, brands which help them express themselves. A person who has achieved financial success will buy a Rolex watch, or drive a Mercedes Benz, for example. Personality is such a strong attraction that companies invest huge amounts of time and money into building and maintaining strongly projected personalities. But the key to branding through personality is making sure that the target audiences see and relate to that personality, and this depends on their perceptions.

One way to find out what these perceptions are is to ask people to describe how they can describe them in personality terms. If we ask them to describe two famous hotels, they might say that the Savoy Hotel in London is an experienced, dignified, elegant, and reliable person, while they might see Singapore's Raffles Hotel as rich, artistic, aristocratic, and somewhat aloof. Personality is not confined to products and companies either, and can be used to project the identity of destinations and countries also. For example, Singapore uses personality characteristics when branding itself as a destination. When it was updating its identity for tourist purposes in 1996, it embodied the words innovative, enterprising, and confident in its promotional material.

There is one more reason why personality is, and will become, increasingly important as years go by. No matter how a personality is chosen, expressed, or visually represented, it is very important to establish this because without it there is little opportunity to differentiate your identity from those offered by others. Personality provides the only long-term solution to differentiation because human attributes are the only ones that are difficult to copy—unlike technology, service, and product attributes. We are moving into the age of parity, where every company will find it easier to reproduce anything that they see other companies have which is desirable. The only thing they will not be able to copy is personality.

However, personality on its own does not produce a strong brand image. It is how this personality is perceived that makes or breaks the image of the product. In other words, personality does not make an impact on people's minds until it is exposed and recognized as being in some way unique, and this is the job of strategic positioning.

Strategic Positioning

Positioning is the other pillar of a brand's strategic platform. It is how personality, in the form of core brand values, is projected to the outside world. Someone can have a great personality, or a company can create a unique personality for itself or its products, but unless people see it and perceive it as such, it will have little effect. Conversely, positioning can be much more successful if it is personified, because personality is a differentiator in itself.

Getting people to like the personality and feel it is right for them is the real task of positioning. To achieve this, knowing who you are aiming at is vital, and the best way to position a personality is to match it with that of its target audience *in their minds and in their experience*. Virgin Airlines, for example, provides product differentiation in live music, free ice-creams, baseball caps, massages, and other services that they know a particular group of target customers will appreciate, thus creating the experience that matches their lifestyles and attitudes. On some of its aircraft it now has complete bedroom suites with all self-contained facilities available for a more affluent market segment. The unorthodox and innovative personality of Virgin is reflected in everything the company does or offers. The brand name itself is somewhat unorthodox for the pinstripe, stiff-upper-lip business world; it also lacks corporate elegance. The Virgin identity is very much a reflection of its founder Richard Branson, whose own entrepreneurial anti-establishment spirit and image heavily influences the Virgin identity, attracting customers who share the same values. The strategic direction he gives to the company by taking on the giants of the airline, financial services, and other industries reinforces the positioning, and the powerful position allows Virgin to enter into totally unrelated fields of business. But there are limits to extending brands. Even Virgin has not been too successful with other ventures such as selling cosmetics. Brand extensions like these are described later in this chapter.

BRAND POWER AND POSITIONING POWER

Positioning shapes and builds the personality, and allows for flexibility in creating different images for different audiences. Without strategic positioning brands cannot succeed.

By looking at two of the brand examples referred to above we can see how powerful positioning can be achieved. With Milo, a Nestlé chocolate-based drink given different names in some countries, the brand is presented in advertising commercials with young, healthy children winning races, scoring goals, and generally enjoying not just the drink but success as well—those 'winning moments'. Energy abounds and one or both parents are there to share the success. For the last few decades the commercials and print advertisements have been the same, including the colours of the brand and the logo. The freshness of the brand is delivered with high technology photography, and the children wear modern sports wear in modern sports surroundings. Consistency of the personality is always present—it would be very difficult to copy successfully, even though the product

itself could be. So the power of the Milo brand comes in its positioning and the strategies used are:
- Rational — nutritious drink
- Benefits — health and energy
- Emotion — winning, success, parental happiness
- Aspiration — children wanting to be like their sports heroes
- Target user — families (adults and children)

Marlboro, by contrast, shows its characteristics of strength and independence through aspirational and emotional strategies aimed at men. The strength is shown through the tough-looking Marlboro man, strong horses, big mountains in Marlboro country, and strong red and white packaging. Independence is portrayed through the Marlboro man who essentially is a loner, the wide-open American plains, and other Western imagery. Marlboro does not talk about its cigarettes—it just positions a personality in the minds of its chosen target audiences. To reinforce the masculinity and personality of the brand, advertisements are supported by sponsorships with sports such as Formula One motor racing. Synchronized swimming would not be appropriate for this brand.

Another example is Guinness. This company now divides up its target audiences according to needs (target-user driven strategy) and positions itself to project the desired image. Different customers might have different needs such as the need to enjoy oneself, to reward oneself, to be sociable, to drink on special occasions, to enjoy a specific taste, to be seen as different, to be patient. Guinness advertising addresses many of these needs in a crowded market-place. But however much these needs differ, and whatever advertising is used to address them, the company never steps away from its core values and its true identity. A Guinness is a Guinness but to an older man it might be described as an old friend, to a lady something velvety, creamy, smooth and nutritious, and to a younger person a big, strong drink. Whatever language or imagery is chosen for whatever audience, the essence of the brand is never threatened, nor is the product changed. Guinness knows the value of strategic positioning and has used it to access and penetrate many new markets over the last twenty years.

POSITIONING HELPS BRANDS AVOID THE COMMODITY TRAP

The basic aim of positioning is differentiation. If people cannot see anything different or unique about what is being offered to them, then economic factors like price come into play, dominating consumer thinking and decision-making. In other words, the products and services find themselves in a commodity situation. A commodity situation exists when potential buyers see nothing special about a product or service that could convince them to choose it rather than competitive offerings and pay a higher price.

Figure 5.2 demonstrates what strategic positioning can do to change this situation and lift a brand out of the commodity trap. How does strategic positioning do this? The skill of strategic positioning is to focus people's minds not just on the tangible but also on the *intangible* values of the brand in question. These could include the brand personality discussed above, or the associations of prestige, status, quality, and other items of value and attraction to the consumer. Positioning creates a powerful image that is perceived as being different, better, and more desirable than the images generated by other brands. The end result for the company is seen in its ability to charge higher prices, and gain premiums

FIGURE 5.2
Differentiation Through Strategic Positioning

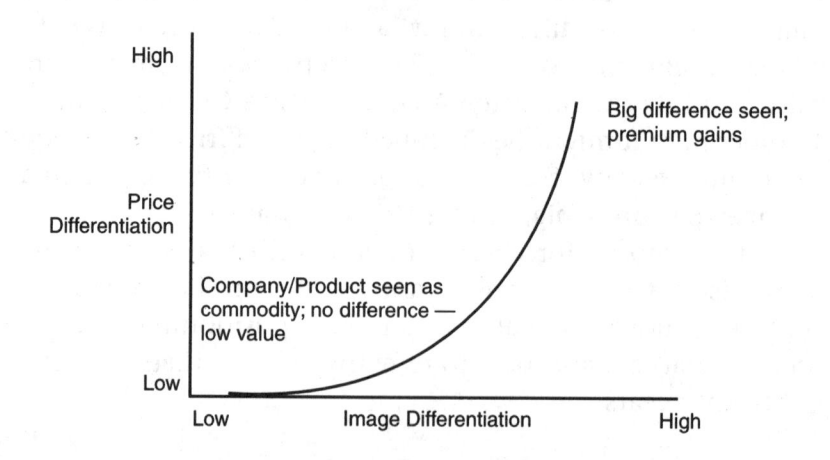

far in excess of delivered cost. The greater the perceived differential value seen by consumers, the greater the premium gains tends to be. To illustrate this, simply ask yourself why many people pay a thousand times or more for a Rolex watch than for a very cheap brand of watch which will keep time just as accurately. That gap represents the strength of the Rolex positioning in the minds of its target audience.

This need to rise out of the commodity trap assumes that premium pricing and product prestige are key objectives associated with brand strategy, but not all companies, of course, pursue such a strategy. Cost leadership, for instance, can lead companies to accept the commodity situation and adopt a low cost–high volume strategy that can also be successful. Nevertheless, with this strategy companies will also rely on establishing a good position in people's minds, one that persuades them to make their brand the preferred choice amongst several other low-cost offerings.

Some companies manage to successfully combine the two strategies, achieving the distinction of having low delivered costs of production and pricing that allows for good margins. Marks and Spencer is a noteworthy example of this, with low costs obtained via its subcontracting policies and a positioning based on quality and value for money.

Sitra Wood, a smaller company in Singapore, has shown that you do not need to be big, or in the retail sector, to be successful in differentiating your company from others in a commodity market. Manufacturing laminated and other timber-based products, it is positioned as a service provider to its customers and suppliers, and has built this position and its brand by doggedly pursuing its principles, which are:

- Highest possible quality of products through use of latest technology
- Developing 'partner relationships' with suppliers and buyers
- Communicating with every supplier and buyer individually, instead of as a homogeneous mass
- On-time delivery
- Constant introduction of new product ranges
- Training of staff to be attentive, responsive, flexible, adaptable, organized, calm under pressure, and giving personal service to deliver on the promise of the position.

These and other initiatives have enabled the company to

become different and better than the competition, and win many international entrepreneurial and marketing awards for its chief executive officer and founder, Roland Chew.

POSITIONING FOR EQUALITY

Time passes quickly, and people's wants, needs, and aspirations change over time. Sometimes you just have to accept the fact that you are falling (or already are) behind the pack, and have to catch up. You have to convince people that you are with it, not out of touch with the latest trend, up-to-date, contemporary, and can match what others offer. This means positioning for equality—showing people that you are not disadvantaged.

Quite often this type of positioning is concerned with the more basic competitive elements of features and benefits, and keeping up with the needs and wants of the people you are trying to retain or acquire as customers. It is also mostly confined to positioning against the competition in specific product categories, such as personal computers. With this particular product category, the life cycles have shortened so much, that by the time many customers have analysed which particular brand's features and benefits will both do the job and give value for money, the next range of upgraded models will have already made the choice obsolete. In such circumstances, positioning is directed at giving your customers the message that you have the necessary elements to be a legitimate competitor in that specific area of interest. So as a computer manufacturer or retailer you have to have models with the latest chips, hard disk sizes, memory capacities, speed, and so on.

POSITIONING FOR SUPERIORITY

Everyone likes to be superior, the best, everyone's choice, but this position is difficult to create and maintain. It goes far beyond equality positioning by seeking to create inequality, a differential advantage, an image of being a cut above the rest, an undisputed leader. Some companies have already done this and several of the world's leading brands come to mind. Others have it firmly placed on their boardroom agenda. With a product, the traditional way of positioning for superiority has been a Unique Selling Proposition (USP), a point of strength which no competitor can match. It is somewhat difficult nowadays to achieve this and more difficult to hold on to it as technology makes replication much easier. USP has also been used to represent Unique Selling Personality, and many companies now are trying to put personality into their products to position them differently, as Land Rover has done with their Discovery model. Companies are also succeeding in building unique personalities from themselves.

Upmarket brands have tried to build up and position themselves on superiority, such as Rolex and Versace. To a great extent they have succeeded, but are always open to attack, even if the position is a strongly held one over time. With the younger generation of people who have acquired wealth for instance, Tag Heuer as a preferred brand is replacing Rolex, because it is positioned as an active, disciplined, professional, risk-taking achiever. In sum, it projects success to a more youthful audience.

Positioning for superiority is only achievable once the target audience acknowledges equality. In other words, you have got to demonstrate that you are at least as good as the competition with whatever it is you are offering, and only then can you persuade people that you really have something extra or special to give.

Companies that gain a superior position can be said to have achieved an SCA or Sustainable Competitive Advantage, being the most preferred choice in their field of competition. Politicians and entertainers are often in the equality zone, and most never get out. The key to success for them is finding an indisputable point of difference that can be used to establish a position of superiority. Mariah Carey's combination of spectacular voice and good looks is a good example of a talented entertainer well positioned for superiority. And once you have established yourself and your image, the search must continue for further opportunities to reinforce that position in the minds of the public. For example, Celine Dion secured the role of singing the title song from the biggest film box-office hit of 1997, *Titanic*. The smart move here was linking a personal position to a major event, and it would not be surprising to see that artiste repeat the strategy with another blockbuster event, in the same way the three tenors have linked themselves to world sporting events, such as the World Cup and the Olympic Games.

MULTI-POSITIONING

It is possible for one brand, company, or product to have many 'faces' or positions, and be attractive to many customer groups. For instance, cars can be 'flexed' via features such as engine capacity, coupé versions, and others. Banks can be positioned broadly but be promoted differently to retail, corporate, small- and medium-sized enterprise (SME) entrepreneurs, public sector institutions, and others. Drinks such as Schweppes soft drinks are 'flexed' via different products such as mixers, mineral waters, fruit and health drinks, with many flavours to appeal to adults and kids, but all of these remain true to the company's basic positioning of quality soft drinks.

So it must be emphasized that any company or product can only have one true, strong position, but it can be tweaked, adjusted, and flexed to emphasize particular strengths or values to attract different customer groups, as long as it is not 'stretched' too far. The amount of 'stretch' available is contingent upon knowledge of various market segments. So multi-positioning can also be seen as line or brand extension, but there are limits to this possibility and you have to know how far you can go.

Harley-Davidson has been successful in marketing its apparel range because it fits well with the needs and desires of the target audience, and the true personality and positioning of the brand. The Harley buyers are attracted by the associations of freedom, patriotism, heritage, and macho attitude, and the accessories and clothing add value to the consumer experience. They are appropriate to the positioning. But even power brands have their limits. The Nike product brand extension from footwear to sports apparel was found to be acceptable, but the step from sports apparel to casual wear was not, because the casual wear segments did not strongly associate with the true Nike position of athleticism, and just getting out there and doing it. Similarly, Johnson and Johnson's Baby Shampoo transferred from babies to 'kids' well, but when tried with adults it did not really make the cut.

Brand and Line Extensions—Possibilities and Difficulties

The dividing line between success and failure in extensions can be thin and somewhat unpredictable, as many companies have discovered. For instance, Cadbury—the famous chocolate manufacturer—has successfully introduced new brands such as Time Out and Whispa Gold in the last few years, but has had failures like Aztec and Rumba. The company has found out that the issue is not whether the taste is good or not so good, but whether new products are *sufficiently distinctive to be accepted* into the consumer's regular repertoire. Cadbury now spends more effort in trying to understand consumer perceptual maps, so that the gaps in the positions between products can be filled meaningfully. Cadbury is sensibly using positioning techniques to help avoid costly mistakes. The key to extension success is to find the spaces in consumer minds and fill them with new brands that will be acknowledged as relevant and different.

Functional and Representational Associations

Another concept that may be helpful when considering extensions is that brand extensions can be thought of as being different from line extensions. The easiest way to describe this difference is to say that brand extensions involve the use of an existing brand name to move into a new product or service category, while line extensions use the existing name to offer a new product or service in the same category. The Mercedes 'A' class is an example of the latter, and Calvin Klein the former.

Brand extension into another category can be achieved if the brand name has powerful associations, and the different businesses are interrelated. Calvin Klein has moved into home furnishings and accessories, but these have all to do with fashion. The clothes designer argues that it is logical to take fashion into the home, and add to and refresh your home wardrobe as you would with your clothes. His aim is to help people create a total lifestyle, and as increasingly more people work from the home, this is even more appropriate. His brand extension is relevant because it is about style, taste, a point of view.

Another way to analyze the issue of extensions and their effect on positioning is to look at the nature of the brand in terms of consumer associations, and whether the marketing strategy is to move the brand up or down with respect to associations of price and quality. Many brands are either functionally or representationally related in people's minds. For instance, a Rolex represents more than just a watch to buyers and occupies a position that is associated with high price, quality, status, and prestige. Casio, on the other hand, has a position linked only to functionality—low price with enough quality in terms of reliability and durability to do the job it is supposed to, but with little association of status or other intangible benefits.

If you want to extend a prestige brand the only possibility is downwards, but a step-down positioning via a product bearing the same name and with lower quality and price will almost certainly damage the original brand with its existing customer base, even though it might attract a newer clientele who aspire to own that brand. So although there is a lot of room for positioning new brand extensions with a prestige parent brand, and the rewards can be substantial, great care must be taken to predict whether there will be any dilution or damage to the core brand image. This is the risk, no doubt calculated, that Mercedes has taken with its new 'A' class. The further down the quality/price continuum the extension occurs, the greater the damage to image is likely to be.

Functional brands are not positioned as high quality items and so there is less room to extend downwards, and any new product introductions will have associations closer to the original brand than would be the case with representational brands. The result of this fact is that extensions are likely to inflict less damage to the brand image. The downside here is that because there is less distance between the brands in terms of quality perceptions, cannibalization of sales for both products may occur through customer confusion. Introducing an extension of a functionally oriented brand and positioning it as higher in terms of quality, and adding status and value to it would be a difficult task, as consumer perceptions will be locked on to the existing brand image.

Distancing of Extensions

One of the ways companies can extend their brands upwards is by distancing the original brand from the extensions through careful positioning. The degree of distancing can be varied and in some cases extreme. The Toyota functionally oriented brand had to leave its name totally out of the picture in order to introduce position a new product, Lexus, in the status and prestige category. This successfully created a luxury brand without the more down-market associations of its other products. For brands already positioned at the high end of a market, the distancing must not be too great, as this will eliminate all the positive associations of the strong core prestige brand name. In such cases, communications strategies must focus on relating the new product to the favourable aspects of the core brand. Too close a positioning, however, may damage both, again through the cannibalization process. The brand manager's task is not an easy one in the field of brand extensions, and positioning is critical to success.

The bottom line for multi-positioning then is that you cannot step away from your basic position or proposition as long as the brand name remains the same, because consumers judge perceptually whether there is a good 'fit' or not between the brand itself and the extension of the brand. Although the discussion above has concentrated on the most common elements of quality and price, this judgement takes into account other elements of importance such as usage occasions. It is for this reason that some companies are forced to step away from the main brand name and create a product that stands alone. Coca-Cola has done this with several products. Others play down the brand name of the company to give the product minimum association with the parent. Launching new products and positioning them with highly individual profiles, while retaining subtle usage of brand equity from the parent, as Levi Strauss did with Dockers, can be a successful strategy. This would probably not have been the case if it were positioned as another product line strongly endorsed by the same major brand.

POSITIONING A NEW BRAND PRODUCT IN AN OLD CATEGORY

Entering a new product category can be difficult because perceptions are so entrenched. For example, detergent manufacturers are now trying to market laundry-soap tablets to people that for years have been used to powders and liquids, but they are finding market acceptance difficult. In the United States, they have not been well accepted, but the major companies are still trying hard to promote them in Europe. The positioning appears to be based on the product attribute/benefit of the tablet itself, with the attribute being the compact size of the tablet and the consumer benefit the fact that consumers no longer have to scoop, measure, or pour. The target market is principally younger working people and small households who essentially do not like doing laundry, and want to minimize the time they take having to do it.

Unfortunately for the companies concerned, people appear to want the option to vary the amount of the ingredient to suit the relative dirtiness of the clothes to be washed. The positioning problem lies in convincing people of the benefits of convenience and time-saving, and has been compared in similarity and difficulty terms to the problem encountered by the proponents of the teabag in the 1950s. Teabags—a comparable situation—eventually took off, but not without considerable investment in educating the consumer. When perceptions are deeply entrenched, companies must be prepared for lengthy and costly campaigns. In this case it might be that research has asked only one of the two vital questions necessary to establish consumer acceptance—'Do you like it?' and not the other one, 'Would you buy it?'

STRATEGIC POSITIONING AND THE BRAND EXPERIENCE

Strategic positioning can create the best of images in people's minds, but it can easily be destroyed if the company or product fails to deliver on the promises made. For a brand's reputation and image to be maintained at a consistently high level, the interaction between the brand and the customer must also be at the highest of levels. For many companies this means attention to detail such as quality control.

Consistency is important for customers, which is the reason Nestlé tests millions of samples of each product in each country each year. Sony says it has built its brand reputation and image on quality and service. The customers' experience of the brand is what really counts.

Brand experience also reinforces a powerful position. If I say I am the only athlete who can win both the 200-metre and the 400-metre races at the Olympic Games when no other person in history has ever achieved it, my reputation is gone if I do not perform well enough. I am just a good athlete with a big mouth. Michael Johnson said it and proved it. The thousands of people who saw the event live, and the millions who saw it on television, enjoyed that amazing experience. For many months he was 'positioned' by agents, media, peers, and Olympic officials as the man who *would* do it. The pressures were enormous but the performance was achieved. The positioning he has now achieved is one of greatness, and millions of youngsters and adults from all over the world look up to him as one of the 'gods' of athletics. His biography publication reinforces his modest character, but fiercely competitive attitude, and tremendous determination to win in the face of adversity, overcoming many huge disappointments. He is now positioned as a role model for kids to follow. By contrast, the once great football hero Maradona found the pressures all too much, fell from grace, and lost his position as a superstar.

Today, the pressure on companies is enormous but the performance must still be there. Failure to give customers what they *expect* can mean failure for the organization itself, and customers expectations are often driven by the power with which companies, products, and people are positioned.

STRATEGIC POSITIONING AND BRAND LOYALTY

There has been a lot of discussion in recent years as to whether or not brand loyalty is decreasing. A lot of money has been invested in market research also to conclusively prove one way or another what is happening. In sum, it does appear that brand loyalty is decreasing to some extent. Studies now show that, within a particular product category (such as cereals) consumers are becoming less particular as to which of the leading two or three brands they will choose. In other words, consumers are generally loyal to top brands, but not necessarily to one of them. The situation appears to be worse if companies generate inconsistent advertising and promotion that give rise to an unclear position and fuzzy image. This has resulted in major companies paying a lot of attention to how they manage their product positioning in categories, and mapping consumer perceptual space to find out how they are categorized on the main dimensions related to consumer decision-making. With cereals, for example, positioning can be decided on the dimensions of healthfulness, taste, or a combination of these. In other words, within a broad category there can be several subcategories available that enable companies to differentiate their products, and add more products into subcategories, thus helping to minimize loyalty issues.

It also appears that people are looking more towards relationships with individual brands as opposed to product performance and value for money. Where once the latter items used to be differentiators for consumer choice, they are now regarded as necessary standard parts of the package. Consumers are demanding more of the intangible benefits that go to make up the brand 'experience' and so the role of product and corporate personality is assuming greater importance. People still want and expect good performance, but into the value equation steps personality and relationships. Gaining loyalty through these elements depends on good positioning.

Whichever way you look at it, strategic positioning is important to stop erosion of brand loyalty, and to ensure the preferred choice in a category or subcategories.

Loyalty Segmentation

A useful way of looking at brand loyalty is a categorization that divides consumers into four groups, namely:
- Loyals who are very committed to the brands they buy, and who will look around until they find their preferred brands.
- Habituals who are loyal through habit but who might defect to other brands if their preferred brands are not available, or if powerful communications from other companies force them to think about alternatives.

- Variety Seekers who are multibrand buyers, wanting variety for its own sake rather than being deliberately disloyal. They still buy preferred brands but may switch if there is unavailability, if they want to use a different brand for a different occasion, or if they see something they perceive to be equal or better in quality.
- Switchers who are only temporarily attached to a particular brand and are influenced by pricing and promotional initiatives.

One of the implications of this for positioning is that companies should try to find out how many of which group it has through research, and what composition the competitors have. Secondly, marketing and positioning strategies should be aimed at reaching and influencing all groups to minimize defection. Loyals and Habituals could be rewarded by the introduction of loyalty programmes. Variety Seekers and Switchers could be shown the adaptability of the brand to multi-usage situations, and Switchers could be tempted to stay with long-term promotional campaigns. The main task for the brand manager is to vary the marketing mix according to the brand portfolio and its loyalty composition with a view to:

- Keeping and acquiring Loyals
- Stopping Habituals from straying
- Providing more perceived variety for Variety Seekers
- Minimizing the number of Switchers

Decisions will have to be made between long-term brand investment in terms of product development and advertising, and the short-term impact of tactics such as temporary price concessions and promotions. These are not easy decisions to make and care has to be taken not to damage the brand image, but brand management aimed at increasing the lifetime value of customers is becoming more important as loyalty is seen to decrease. More discussion of this topic is included in Chapter 9 under Relationship Marketing.

CO-BRANDING AND POSITIONING: REWARDS AND RISKS

Brand partnerships have increased over the last few years in an effort by many companies to keep visible in as many ways as possible. Co-branding is the joining together of brands to reach target audiences of mutual interest. As co-branding is dependent on shared communications it stands to reason that positioning strategies also have to be shared, and so co-branding is also sometimes referred to as co-positioning.

Sometimes joint branding campaigns are more of a temporary arrangement for a specific sales promotion campaign. This can be enormously successful as both McDonald's and Disney have experienced when teaming up together on promotional items, the most recent example being characters from Disney's huge movie success *A Bug's Life*. McDonald's also did this with the syndicated Snoopy character introducing twenty-eight international Snoopys dressed in different national costumes for sale with Extra Value Meals as collector items.

Some companies advertise the success of the partnerships. Computer Associates have recently done this telling readers how their software has helped the West McLaren Mercedes Formula One motor racing team, featuring the endorsement of Ron Dennis, the Managing Director of McLaren International, and Mika Haakinen. Oracle has done the same, describing in advertisements how it has helped Kellogg's to streamline its operations.

By contrast, some companies have tried joint brand ventures involving the development of completely new products, as with Nestlé and Frito Lay via Pretzel Flip, a pretzel coated with milk chocolate, the Mercedes Benz and Swatch 'smart car', the JavaOS business operating system jointly produced by technology giants IBM and Sun Microsystems, and a product developed by Eastman Kodak Company and Intel Corporation to bridge traditional photography with digital imaging centred on film 'digitization'. Intel has also collaborated on new chip architecture with Hewlett-Packard that will result in a new product called Merced. Citibank has sealed a powerful partnership with Netscape to market financial services on the Internet, which Netscape unashamedly says it hopes will strengthen its brand through the association.

Companies offering relationship marketing loyalty programmes involving cards for consumers have been the pioneers of co-branding, and developments in this field are emerging all the time. For instance, Standard Chartered Bank and the distributors of Nissan cars in an Asian country have joined together with Visa to offer a product called The Nissan Advantage Visa credit card which not only gives Nissan car owners benefits such as discounts for spare parts and price reductions on services, but also a credit facility to pay for them. Tesco in Britain has also enjoyed a great deal of success linking its Club Card with several suppliers of goods and services.

The reasons for co-branding include:
- Access to a wider customer base, new customer acquisition, and increased market share
- The opportunity to add more value to customer transactions through offering additional benefits, services, and products
- Shared development, ownership, and marketing costs including distribution, advertising, and promotion
- The enhancement of customer loyalty

Getting the package right can bring big profits, but there are risks which need to be carefully considered, namely:

1 Finding a good brand 'fit'. Different brands have different image power and appeal to different audiences. While the prospect of gaining access to another brand's customer base is attractive, it might not be the right kind. It may be too downmarket or for the wrong age group. For brands occupying a powerful position with their own customers, linking their names to others may be advantageous or detrimental to current perceptions. Will the move dilute the current positioning and brand equity? Rolex and its sponsorship of a major sporting event like Wimbledon is a good fit, but Armani would not fit with soccer, because the self-esteem of Armani purchasers and the exclusivity positioning would be hurt.

2 Connected to this is the problem of how the different advertising tones and styles employed by the separate brands can be adjusted to become complementary, without losing individual consistency. As these elements are crucial to personality projection, is it possible or even desirable to bring two or more brand personalities together? Personality clashes should be avoided at all costs. At the same time, keep in mind that changing personality can be disastrous to brand loyalty.

3 Will the customer see real added value? The customer

experience is the other critical issue, and it is important to test out whether they see the linking of brands as a real attempt to offer them more value, or just a gimmick to help the companies concerned boost sales. They do ask the question 'What's in it for me?', and the resultant perceptions will make or break the initiative.

The temptation to co-brand/co-position could cause permanent damage, and so any major initiatives in this direction should be carefully thought through strategically and tested out with customers.

BRAND GUARDIANSHIP

Vital to the building of a strong brand and a powerful position is protection of the brand. If a brand personality has been created it must be executed in a consistent manner. In other words, the positioning process, if projecting the personality through advertisements, sales promotions, public relations or whatever, must never step out of character. If the personality is seen to be changeable, people will no longer have trust in the product or company, just as they would feel if a friend or boss were in a different mood every day. It is therefore of crucial importance that every communication appearing before consumers is examined closely to ensure that the personality of the brand shines through, and that the messages are in line with the strategic position.

The importance of guarding the brand is why many companies are very reluctant to substantially change even logos and names, because consumers identify so strongly with them. Corporate personalities also need protection; the positioning can be undermined if the employees customers interact with do not act in the way that the positioning has presented the personality. This means that every company's culture must be changed to fit the personality that the customers have come to expect from communications activities. Unfortunately, many companies fail to realize that brand guardianship has to be taken to these extremes, and as a result the customer experience suffers and damages brand equity.

Companies that have reached world-class brand status usually go to great lengths to ensure that the promise is delivered, and it is not uncommon to see brand guardianship committees in operation that only sign off on any corporate or product communication if the personality and positioning are correctly executed. Additionally, they often conduct substantial organizational development and training initiatives to ensure there is no gap between the corporate identity projected and the customer experience. Brands are profit centres in their own right, and must be nurtured and protected if the returns on investment are to be realized.

THE CHANGING ROLE OF BRAND MANAGEMENT

Since the 1970s, there have been some discernible changes in the role of brand management, and the activities of brand managers. Principally, these changes are seen in a change in emphasis from:

- An industry to a market focus
- Tactical to strategic thinking
- Local to global market focus and analysis
- Product to category management
- Product branding to corporate branding
- Product responsibility to customer relationship responsibility
- Managing brand performance to managing brand equity

Industry to Market Focus

One of the more obvious trends in business has been the movement away from product-led to customer-led marketing. This needs little explanation, but its impact on brand management in one sense has been to force managers to get closer and listen to the customer. This has brought about many initiatives in market research, customer service, and quality management, and it has also meant that brand managers are getting more involved in new product development.

Tactical to Strategic Thinking

Another change has been the movement of corporate strategic thinking from merely looking at how to grow the business within a specific industry, to a mind-set that looks at expansion across many industries and in multiple markets.

This has led brand management into taking a much more strategic view, and it has become a more holistic activity, looking at how to project consistent identities and create consistent images in a variety of different situations.

Local to Global Market Focus and Analysis

The economies of scale required to achieve world-class brands, and the breakdown of market boundaries for reasons explained earlier, have meant that more and more companies are adopting a global focus, and brand management now has to achieve the right balance between global identities and local adaptations. This trend has also led to the emergence of many more strategic alliances, involving co-branding in order to reduce the cost of global reach.

Product to Category Management

Vicious competition in many markets, especially in fast moving consumer goods, has given rise to the management of categories as opposed to individual products, with the brand manager looking at a multi-product portfolio, and a complex set of positioning alternatives. Procter and Gamble, for example, assigns a general manager responsible for profitability to each category it competes in.

Product Branding to Corporate Branding

While product branding continues to play an important part in brand strategy, there has been a marked trend towards corporate and umbrella branding, with even the traditional die-hard product brand organizations like Procter and Gamble bringing the corporate brand more into the spotlight.

Product Responsibility to Customer Relationship Responsibility

Another interesting development has been the move away from the management of product(s) to the management of customer relationships, signified by the fact that some companies are now giving brand managers responsibility for specific groups of customers, across an entire product range. In this respect, brand management is becoming customer management.

Managing Brand Performance to Managing Brand Equity

Finally, companies have now become much more concerned with the total value of their brands as well as profitability. The valuation of brands is by no means an exact science, but the sale of brands for prices far in excess of the asset valuation has meant that brand building has become a business in its own right. For the brand manager, this means that several measures of performance have to be taken into account simultaneously, as brand equity measurement can include a whole host of variables including brand awareness, brand loyalty, perceived quality, price, market share and cash-flow premiums, internationality, support, protection, and many others.

All in all, the above changes mean that brand management is a much more dynamic and complex function than it has ever been, and the challenge for many companies now is to develop the right blend of skills and experience in their managers. What has not changed is the unassailable fact that strategic positioning creates brand excellence, and this arguably remains the most important activity for anyone with brand building responsibilities.

USING THE POWER GRID

Some companies have devised ways of estimating the strength and value of brands, and how they are positioned in comparison to others. While lacking total accuracy, they can be a useful way of assessing the position of your brand and determining future brand strategy. One such instrument is Young & Rubicam's Brand Asset Valuator. This does not value your brand in dollar terms as some other methods claim to do, but it does indicate your brand's position relative to others based on certain criteria. Every two years since 1993, the company has undertaken a major survey of brands, asking consumers questions to reveal

- What they know about them
- How they feel about them
- Whether they use them
- Whether they intend to use them

- Their attitudes towards the media, advertising, and marketing communications
- Information about themselves

The result is a large global database of consumer brand perceptions. Armed with this information, Dentsu, Young & Rubicam use four primary measures to evaluate current brand performance, to identify core issues for the brand, and to evaluate brand potential. These four 'pillars' are used to assess brand strength and brand stature. Brand strength is measured by the two pillars of differentiation and relevance, which estimate its potential for growth. Brand stature is measured by brand esteem and brand knowledge, and estimates its consumer scope and strength.

By plotting brand strength against brand stature, and interrelating all four pillars, the Brand Asset Valuator demonstrates how successful brands can be built, and serves as a useful diagnostic tool for brand strategy and positioning. The resultant Power Grid is shown in Figure 5.3.

Quadrant A tends to contain new brands that, quite understandably, show low scores on all four levels of differentiation, relevance, esteem, and knowledge. If you are in this

FIGURE 5.3
The Power Grid

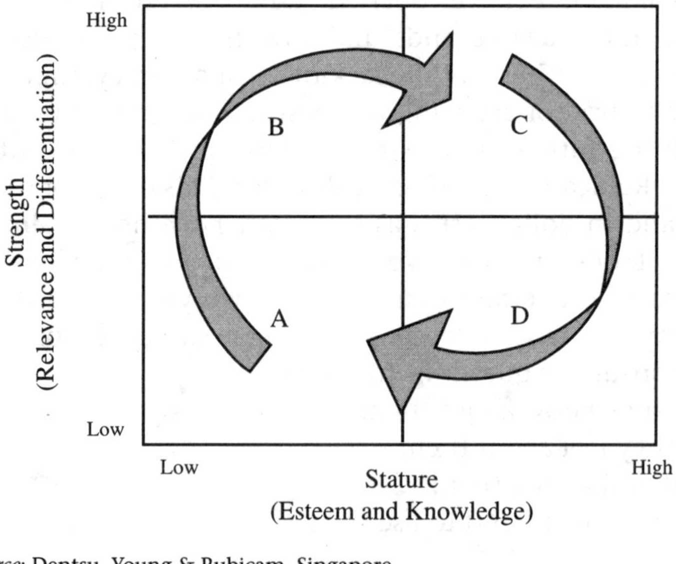

Source: Dentsu, Young & Rubicam, Singapore.

sector you will have to work hard on differentiation and relevance, but the brand will not yet be held in high regard or be widely known.

If you are in Quadrant B, strength of the brand has risen considerably, and the opportunities are very good for brand development. Differentiation and relevance are still building and the main challenge is to develop esteem for the brand. Niche brands often occupy a space in this quadrant, and are often successful. This quadrant represents a tremendous chance to leverage consumer perceptions so that brands are more accessible to the consumer.

If you find yourself in Quadrant C, your brand building effort has been very successful. First, the brand has strong esteem, probably being perceived as very high quality, and it is popular. Also, the overall level of knowledge is increasing, indicating that the brand is truly understood by large numbers of consumers. Through vigilant marketing, a brand's strength and position in this sector can be perpetuated by continual management of its strength. Relevance and differentiation are also high. Effective brand management is needed here to avoid decline, for example, by keeping attitudes.

Finally, Quadrant D represents the trouble spot for brands, and is an indicator of eroding potential. If scores for differentiation and relevance are slipping, the likely consequence of this is a fall in esteem. This signals that good brand management is lacking, and without further attention the brand could slip back into Quadrant A. The brand is unfocused, and consumer perceptions are showing that they find it much less differentiated and relevant to them. If left unattended, the brand will lose its esteem and possibly fade from consciousness.

With the Power Grid, you can pinpoint the position where your brand lies, and make decisions about its future. The high and low scales range from 0 to 100 per cent, so your brand's position is located precisely. If positions for many brands are plotted (which the company does for countries), then a scatter diagram is produced. It can be configured for various forms of segmentation, and shows not only what perceptions have positioned a brand, but also what needs to be done to get the brand where it needs to go. As with any research tool, it is important to remember that markets and relative positions are dynamic, and so the data generated must be used as a help towards strategy formulation, and not as the sole determinant of it.

Case Study

BRITISH AIRWAYS: TURNING ON THE POWER OR LOSING THRUST?

The airline industry is extremely competitive, with massive pressure on companies to drive down costs, fly on more routes, and attract more passengers. Rationalization is a feature, and globalization is no longer an option but a necessity. Consequently, airlines are linking up through mergers, acquisitions, joint ventures, code sharing, and other strategic alliances in an effort to stay in the race. Customers are becoming more demanding. The basic elements of flying are still required—safety, timeliness, and others—but customers now look to greater degrees of comfort and service than they have ever done before. Faced with a market situation like this, how can strategic positioning help build the brand?

British Airways's (BA) desired consumer perception since 1983 has been 'The World's Favourite Airline'. It did not occupy this position in consumer minds at that time but has more or less achieved this over the last fifteen years where it is now rated consistently at or near the top of the airline charts. BA is regarded as a major global airline, and regards itself as the industry leader in many ways.

However, recognizing that a brand must continually develop, BA did some research to find out more about their customer base and what they wanted. The results were interesting. They found that over 80 per cent of customers travelled internationally and 60 per cent were from outside Britain. Moreover, customers basically wanted the airline to be more open-minded and culturally aware, less formal, more modern, more caring, and more innovative. A tall order.

Coupled with this message, a new mission has been generated 'of becoming the undisputed leader in world travel'. Like all worthwhile mission statements there has to be an explanation and in this case, the meaning of the words is as follows:

Undisputed	—	'remaining clearly ahead of the field, setting standards for others to follow'.
Leader	—	'first in terms of innovation, serving customer needs, and financial performance'.
World Travel	—	'focus on international routes, build global alliances, and diversify from the traditional airline business into world travel-related areas'.

To enable all these to happen, BA is going to invest heavily—an overall £6 billion in fact, which will cover a complete programme including new aircraft and buildings, improved products and services, training for improved customer service, and a new corporate identity.

With the new identity BA is both consolidating its existing position, and repositioning at the same time. Should it bother when it is already successful? Well, keeping up with customer expectations is one thing, but BA wants to grow its brand—it does not want to be just a top airline brand but a true world brand. It also wants to give customers a better total experience because this is the foundation of success for any brand. And it also wants to reflect the cultural diversity of BA itself. In short, it wants to earn 'British Airways a place amongst the élite of the most admired companies in the world'.

Its new brand identity or personality is 'A Citizen of the World'. There is also meaning behind this, of course—BA is saying that it is 'not simply a British Airline with increasing global reach, but an airline of and for the world, born and based in Britain'. It is also saying that it is a company 'passionately committed to serving our customers, and connecting the different communities of the world'.

A new visual identity has been launched most significantly in plane livery. There are new colours that return to those of the British flag to reinforce BA's reputation for safety, security, and professionalism, and link to its British base and background. There is a fresh typeface and a new speed marque symbol (this logo is an evolution of previous ones, modernized to reflect speed and innovation). Advertising campaigns now show people—mainly faces—to reflect its concern for people and the countries it is connecting, as opposed to traditional industry advertising with strong aircraft and technical/product features. Perhaps the most interesting development of all was the commissioning of around sixty pieces of artwork from people around the world reflecting their cultures, and painted on the planes' tailfins, which reinforce the identity and the promise offered by that identity.

BA will also be going into diversified world travel—related businesses such as financial services, traveller publications, and many other activities all designed to enhance the customer's total experience, making it easier for them to arrange all their travel requirements.

BA is an example of how extensive the thinking needs to be when undertaking long-term brand development, and how all-encompassing changes have to be, involving:

- Mission
- Personality and positioning
- Customer research
- Visual identity
- Making things happen for the customer

With strategic repositioning BA hopes to achieve its world-class brand aspirations. On the promotional side, the company says in a recent range of advertisements 'The World is closer than you think', again reflecting its new position and its world brand aspirations. The success of this major rebranding and repositioning exercise will have to be judged by customer response. Some say that the company is trying to move too far away from the identity that customers are comfortable with. There are indications that this could be true. Already the ethnic tailfins are to be replaced as British customers are unhappy. The Union Jack will be used again.

Whether this ambitious brand development programme will succeed also requires the compliance of the BA workforce to deliver the brand personality changes needed. These are quite different from the existing culture, and may meet with some considerable resistance to change.

The jury is out, and we await the result with interest.

Positioning with Focus

World Market Trends Affecting Positioning

If you do not have a target to aim for, the chances are you will not hit anything. This is obvious, but there are still thousands of businesses and millions of people around the world who either fail to establish what target audience they are aiming for, or start off by setting clear targets and then get side-tracked.

This chapter is concerned with identifying precisely who your target audience is. As background, and before we get into the details of how the latest techniques are progressing, it is important to understand the current world market trends which affect this issue and have an impact on strategic positioning. There are six of them, namely:

- Breakdown of Market Boundaries
- Globalization and World Brands
- Increasing Market Fragmentation
- Product Diversity and Life Cycle Compression
- Greater Customer Sophistication
- Electronic Business

BREAKDOWN OF MARKET BOUNDARIES

Traditional market boundaries have been burst wide open, partly by technology that has allowed companies to move into unrelated, formerly inaccessible areas. This has resulted in a lot of industry crossovers, where firms move into new industries. Fujitsu, for example, has described itself as a company whose business is concerned with telecommunications, computers, and micro-electronics, firmly declaring that it is in at least two industries. Also, technology has made available a vast array of substitute products which many companies can produce, for example, cables with enormous channel capacity, high pressure water drills for bone surgery, and plastic springs for car suspension units.

Deregulation has also made a significant contribution, and it is hard to think of any industry where some form of liberalization is not taking place. From financial services to photosystems, medical products to motor cars, every industry is being liberalized as the World Trade Organization (WTO) and other international agreements are put into place. One of the first significant signs of this was the breakdown of the Japanese banking cartel and the entry of Citibank into Japan in the early 1990s. The ASEAN Free Trade Area (A.F.T.A.) and WTO initiatives are now accelerating the pace of deregulation in Asia, and the rest of the world.

Strategic alliances have also given firms access to new markets, for example with airlines. As global presence becomes a necessity for them to achieve volume economies, many airline companies have entered into code-sharing agreements, such as Malaysia Airlines and Virgin Atlantic. Larger alliances are also being established such as the Star network of several airlines. Joint ventures and equity swaps are also providing vehicles for multimarket access.

GLOBALIZATION AND WORLD BRANDS

The transformation of domestic markets into global markets is a compelling trend, and there are some significant forces at work here. For instance, there is a global standardization of buying patterns with consumers the world over buying similar products and services from fashion to fast food, cars to cosmetics, music to medicines. This is fuelling globalization and assisting global players to develop world brands backed up by in-country local strategies (more of this in the last chapter).

The opening up of previously restricted markets like Eastern Europe and former communist countries has also made global marketing easier. Similarly, the rapid advance of technological change has made it relatively easy for conglomerates to co-ordinate far-flung operations, and communicate faster world-wide with many different audiences. The challenge for many of Asia's companies now, as relative newcomers to global marketing, is how to cope with more international competition, get known around the world, and be able to access new markets.

INCREASING MARKET FRAGMENTATION

New customer groupings (market segments) are emerging with their own distinctive needs and wants requiring and getting special attention. For instance the 'Yuppies' segment in China is now estimated at over 100 million people! At the same time, dramatic changes in demography and lifestyles are occurring, together with seemingly insatiable demands for convenience and service. This means that companies have to look more and more into the minds of consumers for views of the future. The bottom line is that these changes are rendering mass marketing obsolete and eroding customer loyalty. So, paradoxically, whilst consumers are tending to buy similar things world-wide, they are insisting on greater customization. Large markets are therefore breaking up into smaller markets demanding variations of generic products and services. Increasingly, new and emerging customer groups are being discovered, giving problems for mass marketing. The trend is towards mass customization, and new techniques of segmentation are being employed to help firms deal with this issue. As an example of this, taking into account all combinations of features and options available, the Ford Motor Company can offer more than 36 million models! People are demanding more and more customization of products.

PRODUCT DIVERSITY AND LIFE CYCLE COMPRESSION

With mass customization comes product diversity, and pressure is on to extend product ranges to keep up with market trends. Life cycles are also getting shorter, being measured now with some categories in months rather than years. With products like washing machines and refrigerators, it was around thirty years before the market reached maturity; with microwave ovens, ten years; and for compact disc players, three years. With personal computers the life cycle is even shorter. Buy now and your machine will be made obsolete by a better model with advanced capabilities within six months.

In addition to this, the crunch for companies is that USPs are increasingly tough to find and keep. It is now extremely difficult for any company to produce a product or service that has something unique about it which cannot be replicated nor even enhanced by competitors in a very short space of time. All of these pressures are giving rise to product proliferation in the search for market gains.

GREATER CUSTOMER SOPHISTICATION

Improved levels of education, changing income distribution patterns, and access to sophisticated international media, mean that today's consumers are more knowledgeable and able to understand even the most technical of products, their differences, and what value they offer. Coupled with this, in many countries of the world purchasing power has risen, fuelled in part by credit facilitation.

Lifestyles have also changed dramatically in fast developing countries like those in Asia, and this is giving rise to changing demand patterns. All these factors have caused consumers to exercise their power of choice more forcefully, and to be more likely to change their loyalties than ever before. Companies will increasingly have to pay greater attention to their changing needs.

ELECTRONIC BUSINESS

As we move into the digital age, the Internet and other sophisticated communications media are forcing us to do business in a different way, much of which is without face-to-face contact with the customer. Some companies are adapting very well to this. Dell Computers, for example, has no sales outlets but sells billions of dollars of its product through direct sales and the Internet. As this trend continues, it poses new challenges for positioning of all kinds. It is much easier to influence minds when there are more tools to use than computer screens. However, these challenges must be faced and overcome.

All six world market trends need careful consideration and when choosing strategies for reaching customers and influencing minds, there are many questions to answer, such as:
- Which markets are we operating in?
- Which markets do we want to operate in?
- Who are our competitors in the markets?
- How can we position ourselves globally *and* locally, while keeping brand consistency?
- Which market segments are growing, declining, remaining stable and offering the most opportunities?
- Which segments are our priorities?

- How can we maintain rapid change in product development and maintain a consistent position?
- How do we talk to sophisticated consumer groups?
- How do we position ourselves when we cannot / do not see the customer?

PROBLEMS AND OPPORTUNITIES

Another way of looking at problems and opportunities that the six trends give for strategic positioning is as follows:

	Problems	**Opportunities**
Breakdown of Market Boundaries	Competitors can move in and perhaps weaken our position.	Extend our position to new markets and widen our customer base.
Globalization and World Brands	We may not have the resources to compete with global players. Will our position be credible?	Find a powerful position that will take us across all cultures and countries.
Market Fragmentation	Establishing multi-segment position but remaining true to a fundamental proposition.	Secure dominant profitable 'niche' segments with a focused position.
Product Diversity	Rapid product development needs high investment in technology and corporate positioning.	Develop line extensions based on current positioning strengths.
Sophisticated Customers	Understanding multi-segment wants, needs, lifestyles, and others.	Develop brand loyalty with powerful positioning.
Electronic Business	Developing trust and confidence in a new market, and projecting our corporate personality.	Establish a powerful position now to gain rapid market share for early entrants.

All of the above issues have one thing in common—hitting the target—and the best formula for most situations is to focus! Greater focus provides a better chance of positioning success.

Giving Focus to Strategic Positioning

It is very difficult, if not impossible, to position something successfully if it is not clear whose minds you are trying to influence. Some good ideas have failed because of this, and failing businesses have been turned around by refocusing.

The classic example of turn around using focus for positioning is the story of SAS which CEO Jan Carlzon inherited in 1981. His new focus for the airline was to make it the best airline for the frequent business traveller. This worked initially and made the airline highly profitable, but when SAS moved away later on from its core business it once again became less profitable.

Even world-famous brands sometimes make the mistake of losing focus. Levi Strauss & Co. did this in the 1970s, moving away from their core product (jeans) into baby clothes, leisure suits, and other items of clothing. The result was damage to their image in the minds of many customers, not to mention a considerable loss of investment. They were really in the business of making jeans and had been for a century or more, so for them it was actually getting back to basics. It took a long time, but having found their way again, the company then did the right things by capitalizing on the brand strength of the name, and positioning itself powerfully again with upmarket jeans products like the 501, revitalizing its image. Now if they want to get into different markets they produce different brands not associated with the Levi's name, such as Dockers.

Club Med is another example. Holidays are holidays, but Club Med saw a gap in the market for young people who wanted to meet other young people and have an active, fun holiday. The product was designed well with non-stop entertainment, originally quite basic accommodation with no telephones, everyone eating together, and payment with beads, not money. The result was a monster hit, but success has changed the concept, and the customer base. The focus was lost in the quest for expansion. Club Med changed to try and compete with luxury resorts, and the customer base changed, now being families and middle-aged people as opposed to young adults. Allowing themselves to lose their position has now put the Club Med chain under financial pressure. Some of the product features still remain the same, but the original target market and the original brilliant idea appear to be somewhat lost, and the company is now trying to revitalize itself.

Cadbury's did a similar thing, by entering into different markets under the Cadbury's name into foods such as Smash (instant mashed potato) and Marvel (milk powder). These had nothing to do with chocolate. To regain focus they were sold off to avoid further dilution of the Cadbury brand name. To consumers, Cadbury is chocolate. Refocusing and some outstanding advertising commercials regained the strategic positioning the company had enjoyed before its diversions.

B.A.T. Industries PLC is divesting itself of its financial services business in order to regain focus on its tobacco side. It regards cigarette manufacturing as its core business and wants to consolidate its global position in this industry. Well-known brand names are so much a part of people's lives that you play around with them at your peril. Hewlett-Packard found out that if they removed their company name endorsing their products that have strong brand names like LaserJet and DeskJet, they could lose up to half their sales!

It pays to remember that you are trying to build perceptions in people's minds, not just in customers or potential customers but in your employees too. If what you are doing is difficult to express, hard to understand, complicated, and lacks focus, the less chance you have of building up a powerful picture in people's minds. Confused product ranges produce confused customers. Choosing a can of peas from a supermarket is not easy because none stand out. Choosing a car from a certain category is complicated by the endless variety of models and features.

Confused communications produce confused images. Some companies have advertisements with nothing but background colour and their name, which means nothing to the consumer. The greater the precision, the greater the chance of success, and the greater the power of positioning. Precision comes from knowing your target audience, understanding their needs and wants, and giving them the messages they want to hear. With this approach it becomes easier to stand out from the crowd.

FINDING FOCUS THROUGH NICHE MARKETING

Companies and individuals often lose focus through complacency, as we have seen, by believing they can put their name to anything and enjoy success. Others never find a focus because they do not understand that the markets they seek to influence are not homogeneous. The rise in importance of niche or target marketing as a technique essential to strategic positioning (by providing and keeping focus) has been marked over the last fifteen years or so. It has also been the driving force behind market segmentation.

As people and markets become more sophisticated and complex, an understanding of them becomes more difficult. One trend already mentioned in world markets is market fragmentation, where mass marketing has given way to mass customization. Another trend, amongst brands, is for one brand to try to occupy different positions in the minds of different target customer groups. The power of the consumer has to some extent forced these things to happen, and accelerated the need for 'niche' or target marketing.

There are several benefits to be gained from niche marketing and focused positioning. First, it would be foolish to ignore the fact that markets are no longer homogeneous, and most companies now accept this view. Secondly, many companies have discovered that niche markets can be less competitive and easier to defend. Indeed, niche markets exist because the wants and needs of the people in them have not been fully recognized and served, so entry itself is an easier task. For the same reason, those enterprises that do understand them and cater for them are often rewarded with substantial profits. Finally, the niche approach allows anyone to win, as size is not a problem. For example, one European chemical company has a 50 per cent share of the world market for its product, but it employs only twenty-five people.

There seems to be no shortage of people seeking the ultimate niche. Some of these are somewhat bizarre, yet possibly very profitable specific undertakings (perhaps that's the wrong word!), as in the case of a North Vancouver entrepreneur who is building a high-rise mausoleum—the largest mausoleum condominium in North America. Some neighbourhood residents have complained but they are not the target market! Taking an upmarket positioning stance, the place will have theme floors for different religions, such as Christians and Buddhists, medals and weaponry for ex-military personnel, and a tropical area with appropriate music for the Fijian community. The Chinese need not worry because a Feng Shui master has already checked the layout and the address of the property is 88. Mourners will be able to watch their beloved being cremated on a pyre overlooking the city. Now that is niche marketing however you view it, and as far as positioning goes, the owner could certainly argue that it is different and better.

Not quite so unusual, but not that far away either, is a restaurant and bar in London called PHARMACY. It is a theme concept, like a Hard Rock Café, but full of bottles, tubes, and other relevant paraphernalia or memorabilia. Staff who serve wear hospital gowns, and your seat might resemble a well-known tablet. Drinks have appropriate names, and so far it is said to have been quite successful, although there have been a few people wandering in to get their prescriptions filled.

Even taxi drivers can niche. Some have fancy cushions, others interesting magazines to read. But someone called Elvis in Singapore uses a luxury Mercedes structured as both a taxi and his mobile office with every conceivable hi-tech item in it. There are stereos, LCD screens, a TV, videos, and so on. Customers experience an entertaining, relaxing ride in an unusual office.

There are many opportunities for niche marketing and positioning, but it all boils down to really understanding what people like and what they will 'buy'. The key to successful niche marketing is market segmentation.

Market Segmentation and Positioning

Dividing up a market into various customer groups that have similar wants and needs is the process of market segmentation, and there are several reasons why segmentation is becoming more important for positioning.
1 Market segments exist because markets are not homogeneous and are fragmenting, so it is not possible to target everyone. Segmentation facilitates the selection of parts of

the market which offer greater appeal. Market segmentation is therefore sometimes called selective marketing.
2 As certain customer groups do have different needs and wants, identifying them provides an opportunity to understand them, and in turn, serve them better.
3 Once identified, segments allow for selection in terms of which offer greater appeal, thus giving rise to the terminology sometimes used: of 'selective marketing'. The appeal of a particular segment could be its rate of growth, its profitability, or its fit with what we want to market. A new 4 × 4 vehicle, for instance, needs a positioning aimed at those people who aspire to fit a certain lifestyle or mode of self-expression.
4 Segmentation gives focus and direction to positioning efforts. The focus gained makes it easier to set clear objectives and measure their achievement against our own targets and the progress of competitors.
5 For smaller companies where niche marketing is mandatory, segmentation provides opportunities to find, communicate with, and defend specific markets.
6 Segmentation allows for the upgrading of customers, as with the credit card market, from ordinary to gold to platinum to titanium.
7 It brings about profitability by helping to avoid the commodity trap, allowing premium prices to be charged. With the help of strategic positioning, quantum leaps in profitability can be achieved.

In sum, market segmentation enables particular target audiences to be chosen, and a suitable positioning strategy be developed. It is virtually impossible to position something or someone without knowing precisely to whom messages should be addressed, and what their expectations are. Because of this, positioning and segmentation are really inseparable.

SEGMENTATION ⟶ TARGETING ⟶ POSITIONING

THE INGREDIENTS FOR SUCCESSFUL SEGMENTATION

Four main ingredients are essential for the success of any segmentation programme.

1 Each segment must behave differently, and must perceive things differently from other groups of people.
2 Each one must be big enough to warrant special attention. There is no point in wasting time and marketing cost in seeking to influence very small numbers.
3 Each one must be accessible for communications and service purposes. It should be possible to prepare a marketing plan for a particular segment that is different from any other.
4 Each segment should have a foreseeable future that is long enough to ensure the required turnover and profitability level is achievable. Segment needs and behaviour do change over time, so this assessment is important for analysing investment returns.

Unless these four criteria are present, it will not be possible to specifically position our messages for them, thus making it very difficult to gain attention and influence their minds.

THE SEGMENTATION PROCESS

There are certain steps to take when carrying out the segmentation process.
1 Choose the variables that mark out a specific group of people from others. This could be determined on the basis of their needs and wants, or how they actually behave. (Examples are given below).
2 Spend time getting to know and understand as much as possible about the segment, or segments if you have identified more than one, and write a profile detailing all the relevant characteristics.
3 Decide on segment priorities, if there is more than one.
4 Decide on what precisely is going to be offered to each segment, what will give to the people in it something better and different from the competition.
5 Choose the most appropriate positioning strategy or combination of strategies that will become the heart of the marketing programme.
6 Write a positioning statement for each segment (see Chapter 7 for details on how to do this).

After going through these stages, there will then be a good platform on which to build the marketing and communications plans. The key to segmentation success, of course, is separating the different segments, and there are many ways of doing this ranging from the simple to the complex. Some of the more interesting ones are mentioned below.

TRENDS IN SEGMENTATION

There are many traditional ways of segmenting markets, such as:

- *Geographic*: by territories like cities, specific localities. This can still be a valid way of segmenting customer groups, for example identifying upmarket housing developments to identify high net worth customers.
- *Demographic*: by separators like age, salary, sex, occupation. One age group having startling growth now and over the next twenty years is older people, as the post-war baby boomers reach retirement age. Some companies see this fast growing market as a great opportunity, as with Anheuser Busch's new light beer Catalina Blonde, which has been developed for that market. Others, like MTV, target young adults, in the age group of 15–34.
- *Geodemographic*: combinations of the above, for example, families of five or more living in a particular suburban area, whose children are all aged under twelve.
- *Sociocultural*: by social class, ethnic group, and even country. For example, Sony Pictures has established key segments of Subteens, Teens, Gen-Xers, Boomers, African Americans, Hispanics, Asians, and alternative lifestyles. The company says 'Market segmentation has become increasingly important in motion pictures at an accelerated pace due to fragmentation of media ... We use market segmentation in the development of our creative materials, and buy different media for different audiences.'
- *Benefits*: by analysing the benefits people expect by being associated with your company, product, self, and others.
- *User behaviour*: by looking at when and why people buy something, how often they use it, on what occasions they use it, and any other patterns of usage. Accord Hotels Division divides consumers into the five main segments of 'Individual leisure', 'Individual business', 'Group leisure', 'Group business' (congresses, conventions, seminars), and 'Airline crew'.

- *Psychographic*: by analysing people's motivations, personalities, attitudes, opinions, interests, and lifestyles. It is this area of segmentation that is of growing importance to strategic positioning, and the remainder of this chapter will concentrate on this.

PSYCHOGRAPHICS: READING PEOPLE'S MINDS

Psychographic segmentation is proving to be more effective for many companies because it is personality oriented, giving an insight into how people think and live their lives. It thus brings us one step nearer to an understanding of their motivations and perceptions. If we look again at the example of credit cards mentioned previously, the premium cards—gold and platinum—cost a lot more and deliver extra services, but research reveals that the real reasons that make buyers of these products spend more are prestige, status, and exclusivity. This understanding of customer thinking gives companies the opportunity to position the higher level cards to appeal to these motivations, and so entice people to upgrade.

Additionally, psychographics analyse personality-type characteristics that tend to be more permanent, and lend themselves to focused positioning and advertising. One of the most respected psychographic segmentation studies is VALS (Values And Lifestyles) 2 developed by the Stanford Research Institute, which isolates eight personality types:

Actualizers
- Enjoy the finer things of life
- Are receptive to new products and technologies
- Read widely
- Are light TV watchers
- Do not place much value on advertisements

Achievers
- Prefer premium products and services
- Are more materialistic
- Read business, news, and self-improvement media
- Are average TV watchers

Believers
- Buy things associated with the 'heritage' of their country of origin
- Are not adventurous in trying out new things

- Read home, retirement, and general interest literature
- Watch TV a lot

Experiencers
- Spend time and money on socializing
- Are impulsive buyers
- Like fashion and the latest trends
- Like popular music
- Are influenced by advertising

Fulfilleds
- Buy a lot of home-related products
- Are not interested in prestige or status
- Read widely and often
- Like education and public affairs programmes

Makers
- Buy basic products and services, not luxuries
- Like buying products associated with value, comfort, durability
- Prefer listening to the radio, and do so a lot
- Like car magazines, outdoor pursuits, and DIY

Strivers
- Have little disposable income, and use credit frequently
- Buy clothes and personal care products
- Are conscious about image
- Do not read a lot, but like TV

Strugglers
- Shop during sales
- Exhibit brand loyalty
- Read daily newspapers, and gender-related literature
- Are heavy TV watchers and like advertisements

Although these are somewhat generalized segments, it is not too difficult to recognize how they can assist the choice of positioning strategies. For instance, it would be of little use to position upmarket fashion accessories to the *Fulfilled* or *Makers* segments via frequent TV commercials, nor would it be a worthwhile investment to try to influence *Achievers* to buy DIY tools for car maintenance through tabloid advertisements. It also brings out the point that not only do different types of consumers have different preferences and needs, they also have different sensitivities with regard to price.

A recent study in China discovered four significant segments among 18–35-year-old working women, giving an insight into their attitudes, opinions, and interests which have implications for marketing. They are:

- *Conventional Women*, who are very traditional and family oriented, like staying at home, watching television, reading newspapers and books, and seldom respond to direct marketing methods. They are less brand conscious than the other segments, rarely buy on impulse, shop moderately, and look for value and product quality more than price and brand names.
- *Contemporary Females*, who carry both traditional and non-traditional values, being career oriented while admitting that a woman's place is at home, and supporting filial piety. They consequently try to combine work and family life, are more brand conscious, less price sensitive, like fashion trends, and are concerned about their appearance.
- *Searching Singles*, who as described are mostly single people who marry late, with modern attitudes to the role of women and a strong career orientation. They read magazines, like fashion and other trends, and regard service standards and store brand image as very important. They enjoy going out with friends, seeing movies, and patronize karaoke and other forms of entertainment, but tend to have lower income.
- *Followers*, who hold moderate views on modern and traditional values, are not very active in social, cultural and physical pursuits. They have limited desire for self-improvement, are less well educated, and are a low-income group.

Lifestyle segmentation is really a part of psychographics, but is often treated as a means of identifying different customer groups in its own right. Lifestyle studies, which concentrate on people's activities, interests and opinions, can also be applied to fast growing and highly specific demographic groups such as the elderly, as shown in one piece of research carried out on their shopping behaviour with respect to over-the-counter drugs. This revealed five segments, namely:

- Family oriented
- Young and secure
- Active retiree
- Self-reliant
- Quiet introvert

There are many other instances in this rapidly growing

area of psychographic research where companies are finding their own categories or typologies from analysing customers specific to their industry. In the personal computer market, Dell Computer formerly segmented their customers according to PC location (home, business, and others), but now has identified five user types:
- Techno-boomers, who have a preference for ease-of-use features
- Techno-to-go-users, who have little patience for sales pitches, and just want a computer in a box
- Techno-teamers, who work as part of a network, and need both the right hardware and software
- Techno-critics, who work in demanding environments where the best available equipment is a priority
- Techno-wizards, who are leading edge users always focused on the newest features

The benefits of the new segmentation to Dell include:
- Better advertising focus
- Ability to develop key promotional messages to fit segments
- Finding gaps in product ranges
- Developing new products to appeal to particular customer groups

There may be sophisticated aspects to segmentation in terms of statistically validating data, but the basis of this is common sense, like most marketing ideas. With market segmentation the idea is to find what specific groups of people want, give it to them, and, if possible, give them a bit more than they expect. Finding out what is and is not important to them is discussed in more detail in Chapter 8.

MASS CUSTOMIZATION, SEGMENTATION, AND FOCUSED MARKETING

The age of mass marketing is gone. Companies can still mass produce but are now forced to enter into the age of mass customization. The main impetus for this phenomenon is the fact that markets are no longer homogeneous but have become more and more fragmented. This trend will continue, and those companies that choose to ignore it will fail, while those that become more focused on satisfying the needs of various customer groups will have greater chance of prosperity.

Market segmentation as a means of dividing up markets is no longer a luxury but a necessity, and the methodology for doing this is now more sophisticated, moving away from traditional quantitative techniques such as demographics to more qualitative means, particularly psychographics. As consumers become increasingly demanding as individuals there is a greater need to understand how different groups of people think, behave, and live their lives. Market segmentation gives both the focus and the understanding to enable companies to improve individual relationships and customer acquisition, and maintain loyalty. The more accurately you can determine the limits of your target audience and understand their thinking, the more powerful your positioning will be.

CASE STUDY

BORDERS—THE LIFESTYLE BOOKSTORE

Borders Group Inc. seems to have found what consumers really want or do not want from a bookstore, and have positioned themselves as the 'Lifestyle Bookstore'. Clearly having done their homework they understand that people do not want a crammed floorspace with clinical, overbright lighting and innocuous piped music. They do not want to feel frustrated by having difficulty in finding types of books they like, nor do they like a lack of choice in their preferred categories. They do not appreciate a lack of comfort with nowhere to sit, or other unfriendly gestures such as shrink-wrapped magazines and books that prevent evaluation of value. In short, they do not like the miserable experience provided by most of the world's bookstores.

Borders understand what people do want when they visit a bookstore, and relate the customer experience to lifestyle. They encourage people to browse amongst a choice of around 150,000 books, minus the shrink-wrapping, so people can see what the content of a possible purchase is, and evaluate the benefit. Customers are provided with comfortable seating in a relaxed atmosphere and can also enjoy food and drink at a café, because Borders understands that many customers have to snatch time in their lunch hour or after work. There is a music section and occasional readings by authors. The result is an altogether more enjoyable experience for those who want to read for leisure, business, or self-improvement.

Borders' positioning backed up by product has made the company a major success in the United States, and the company is now going international with a consistent approach. For instance, customers in its store in Singapore get just the same treatment. Needless to say, Borders is rapidly taking market share from more traditional competitors. It will, however, have to constantly prove to customers that it really understands their needs if it is to maintain its position.

Strategic Positioning and Marketing Communications

POSITIONING STATEMENTS

This chapter deals with some of the alternative ways in which a powerful positioning strategy can be put into action with maximum impact. After having put major effort into finding a credible, workable, achievable position that will satisfy the goals, desired consumer responses, or image to be delivered, it is important that the strategy or combination of strategies is executed well. This will involve developing the key messages to be projected to various audiences, and the most appropriate means of communicating them. But before all that happens, the positioning has to be formalized in one or more positioning statements. This means spelling out the strategy in some detail.

Unless you are in total control of every aspect of image creation, you need to have a communications brief for other people, such as advertising agencies, to follow. This is one of the main reasons for having written positioning statements. If positioning statements are not written there is a real danger that the ideas might be misinterpreted, the strategy not adhered to, and the key messages not expressed clearly. The result will be confusion in the minds of the audience. To keep messages clear and develop a consistent image and position, positioning statements are essential.

Positioning statements are internal documents not meant for public consumption. They summarize strategy, act as a guide for advertising and promotions, and state specifically and briefly what you want people to think about you, your product, or company. They not only spell out the desired image you wish to have, but are a good test for strategy also, as they quickly tell you whether the perceptions you wish people to hold are believable, credible, and achievable. Positioning statements are not easy to write, and often need several attempts. It is best to write them with inputs and agreement from other people. In companies, for example, a corporate positioning statement would need to be considered by as many top and senior managers as possible to gain consensus agreement and buy in, and to ensure execution. Product managers would also need to seek other opinions, and endorsements.

Before writing a positioning statement, it is vital that there is a complete understanding of the following areas:

1 *Yourself, company, product.* This seems obvious but you have to be very clear about what you can really offer that will attract the people you are trying to influence. With products this will mean looking closely at all the features and attributes, and the benefits that people will derive from them. All the time you should be looking for factors that will help differentiate what you have to offer from competitors. You do the same with services. What service standards can you present that will give you the opportunity to suggest a competitive advantage? Companies themselves often have distinguishing characteristics such as global stature, track record, personality, and other unique features that can be highlighted and used as differentiators.
2 *The target audience(s) you want to influence.* Knowing what people need and want is critical, and there is a difference between the two. You might need some food to eat but want a curry. More than that, you might want a vegetarian curry because that kind of food fits in with your belief structure. It becomes important therefore to understand the intangible requirements of people as well as the more tangible ones. Unless there is precision in customer understanding, the messages we send may be irrelevant and lose us credibility.
3 *The competitors you are up against (competitive set).* No strategy is complete without a thorough understanding of the competition, whether you are a football manager, marketing manager, entertainer, managing director, or Prime Minister. Some of the questions to ask might be:
- Which competitors do customers consider?
- What positioning strategies are the competitors using, and why?
- What key messages are they sending?
- What appears to be their competitive advantage and key points of difference?
- Why do customers buy from them?
- What image do they currently have?
- What differences do customers see between them and us?
- What competitor would they switch to if they moved from us?

One of the major problems that can arise here is deciding

just who the competition is. This issue is particularly relevant for fast-moving consumer goods where the definition of categories becomes extremely important, but it does need to be considered in any positioning situation. For instance, if we ask whether or not Michael Jackson is in the category of 'rock music entertainers' we would almost certainly answer yes, but if we ask whether he is competing with the Rolling Stones we would probably say no. Definition of the product category is therefore a critical first stage in competitor analysis, and vital to the positioning effort.

4 *Why you are different and better than the competition.* Analysis of the above areas will allow you to make some accurate judgements as to what position to choose, and which positioning strategy you need to employ in order to influence the perceptions of the target audience(s).

5 *The desired perception you would like to have people think.* Always set a goal in terms of how you want to be seen by people. When you are writing this goal, try to do it using the language of the customer or persons you are trying to influence. If you put yourself in their shoes there is a greater likelihood that you will understand how they think and be successful in managing their perceptions. You will find it easier to track whether you have achieved the intended image or not.

Some of the above analysis might entail commissioned research if you do not have the internal resources to carry it out, and it may take some time, but the quality of your communicated position will end up much more focused and accurate. Once you are ready to write the positioning statement, it has to be done in a concise way.

WRITING AND USING A POSITIONING STATEMENT

There are many ways of writing positioning statements, but they should all contain certain elements. From past experience I have found the following template to be the most practical.

A Positioning Statement Template

COMPANY/PRODUCT/PERSON
is better than

COMPETITIVE SET
(the industry or business you are in)
for

TARGET MARKET
(the customer group or groups you are aiming for)
because it

KEY STRENGTHS
(the total offer you are making to the target audience, particularly its strength)
with the result that

KEY PROPOSITION
(the benefits to be experienced by your target audience)

It is the last two elements of the statement that bring out the answer to the main questions of
- Why are you better?
- Why are you different?

Only if these are answered truthfully and adequately will you be able to persuade customers that you should be their preferred choice. Great care must therefore be taken to ensure that their content is credible, believable, deliverable, and relevant to the wants and needs of the audience whose perceptions you are trying to influence.

With respect to the use of positioning statements, they are internal documents and are not meant for customers. They serve as a guide for employees and agencies involved in marketing the product, brand, or service so that they consistently promote its main strengths.

Developing Key Messages for Different Audiences

While the positioning statements give the overall strengths and focus of what you are trying to tell people, they can be taken further by extracting from them key messages for particular groups of people.

Whether you represent yourself, another person, a product, company, or country, it is most likely that you will want or have to influence more than one target audience. For example, a country might wish to influence the perceptions of, inter alia

- The general domestic public
- Local investors
- Foreign investors
- Foreign governments
- Local media
- Foreign media
- Tourists
- Inter-governmental institutions
- International financial institutions
- Analysts and other specialized commentators
- Domestic and international agencies and pressure groups.

It is highly important that different target audiences are clearly identified, because they will have different needs and wants, different issues of concern, and different perceptions. This means that in order to change their perceptions, different messages will almost certainly be required when communicating with them, but there is still a need to keep to the overall position. For instance, messages for foreign governments might include an item such as a committed bilateral partner.

On the other hand, a message for foreign business companies might promote the existence of a transparent and deregulated environment.

For tourists, clean, green, and scenic places would be the message theme, whereas for students it would be globally recognized qualifications. And so on.

It is somewhat easier for companies with products that have wide appeal to generate one message that is acceptable to all segments. Heinz Tomato Ketchup does this with its 'Slow Pouring' that denotes quality, but for companies wishing to target multiple segments it is a little more difficult, and they may have to vary the communications to do it. The 'Always Coca-Cola' campaign did this by using different musical means such as country and western, rock, rap, and others to reach different audiences, but the overall position remained the same.

With nations it is even more complex, and the overall position may have to be supported by additional messages. So country X may have an overall positioning of a state-of-the-art technology environment, but will vary the messages to investors, tourists, and foreign media to illustrate how that key proposition can benefit each of the target audiences

Whatever form they might take make sure that the messages are communicated to the correct audience who will see them as being:
- Relevant
- Understandable
- Credible
- Interesting
- Motivating

TOTAL COMMUNICATIONS FOR STRATEGIC POSITIONING

There are many options for communicating the position you desire, including:
- Advertising
- Direct marketing
- Sales promotion
- Public relations
- Sponsorships

ADVERTISING

One of the most frequently used components for positioning companies and products is advertising. Advertising is a part of what is called paid mass communications, generally meaning space paid for in a publication, or time on radio, television, or cinema, although it may also be taken to include posters, billboards, and other outdoor advertising. Its main purpose is to persuade an audience to either take some action or develop an attitude towards what is being advertised. Positioning, as we know, is concerned with persuading people that our particular offer is both different and better than similar offers made by competitors, and advertising can be a powerful means of accomplishing this. Some would go so far as to say that it is the best way to position something or someone in people's perceptual space.

Advertising achieves image differentiation mainly through repetition of a particular message, which leads to recognition, recall, attitudes, preferences, and action. It is frequently used by companies but is also becoming more widespread in its application, being a part of national and individual campaigns, where information takes second place in importance to the need for exposure and positive perceptions. A good example of advertising-driven positioning is ABSOLUT VODKA, where the personality of the product (intellect, humour, sophistication) has been consistently marketed and advertised around the world, and positioned in an aspirational way so that it appeals to the target audience in terms of exclusivity.

Advertising can be executed through the various types of media described above, and all have their advantages and disadvantages, but creative repetition is the key to its success. The nature and cost of commercial advertising space means that only a limited amount of information can be placed, and so the frequency of the advertisements is also a governing factor in how effective it is. Little perceptual change will be gained by a limited number of exposures, and often companies complain about the lack of advertising effectiveness when the real reason is that the campaign was too short in terms of the message frequency. Advertising agencies have a constant battle with companies over the length and cost of campaigns because managers often do not understand that it takes time, and a great deal of repetition, for key messages to strike home and change human perceptions that evolve relatively slowly. Image advertising in particular needs a long-term commitment, but when carried out properly with good emotional and creative input, it can be a powerful aid to positioning.

The use of emotion in advertising—appealing to the heart as well as the mind

There is no doubt about it—emotion sells. We hear these words often enough, but why are they true, and how can the use of emotion help the positioning process? Emotion is still a bit of a mystery as far as our understanding of mental processes is concerned, but we do know that it originates in the right brain and manifests itself as a state of arousal. Emotion can also be positive (as in a state of happiness) or negative (as in a state of fear). As far as image is concerned, it is important to establish an emotional relationship with the people who are to be influenced. If positive feelings and emotions can be associated with what we are positioning, there is a much greater chance of attracting people, and altering or producing the perceptions we want people to have.

Emotion is being used a lot more now by service companies who are finding it increasingly difficult to differentiate themselves from each other. Life insurance companies, for instance, are not just talking to consumers about the rational aspects of having a policy in terms of investment and returns, but are using emotional questions and statements in their advertising such as 'What will happen to your family if something happens to you?' and 'We are offering you peace of mind'. Financial services companies are typical of many service organizations trying to persuade consumers that they are different and better than their competitors in markets that are becoming increasingly commoditized. Fidelity Investments in the United States has recently launched a new series of advertisements in an attempt to present the company as being more human and warm, showing shots of their analysts saying why they like to work for the company, and others showing the main character acting in a very helpful way to small investors who need advice. In the age of technology, companies, such as Fidelity, with large dispersed customer bases of millions of people, most of whom they might never meet, have to show that they are not just cold, impersonal, bureaucratic companies, but have a human side that cares for its customers.

Other companies add emotional appeal using safety and security as points of attraction for risk averse consumers, as the Lombard Odier company has done in its advertisement. The main message featured is 'Experienced in the art of asset management' showing an elderly man enjoying painting at the seaside.

An emotional positioning strategy can be used in any industry with success. A BUPA International advertisement uses its tag line of 'A World of Experience in Healthcare' coupled with a message saying 'Even when you're miles away, we'll still be right behind you'. A Hoechst subsidiary, Hoechst Roussel Vet, advertisement carries the parent tag line 'The Future in Life Sciences' with a shot of a happy-looking dog resting its head on its owner's shoulder with the caption 'Imagine your best friend always feeling as good as you do'. The Four Seasons Hotel, Tokyo, pictures a businessman having a morning drink looking out of his window at a lovely garden with the caption 'I need some calm before the storm'. What all these companies have realized is that emotions are powerful feelings that everyone in the world has, and that once awoken can move people to see things and behave differently.

There are many ways in which advertising can bring out peoples' emotional feelings including the use of:
- Drama
- Shock
- Fear
- Humour
- Warmth
- Aspiration
- Music
- Sex

All of these have their advantages and disadvantages, which must be carefully thought through before use, and any agency creative must be examined very thoroughly to make sure that the type of emotion to be used is in line with the overall position and desired image. *Appropriate* is the key word in creative selection.

Drama

Dramatic narrative and visuals can be powerful in positioning. One brand of coffee ran a series of advertisements that showed a young couple who met over a cup of coffee, and followed them as the relationship developed through its ups and downs. It was like a mini soap opera series, and audiences loved it. The coffee was always present, being a part of their everyday lives. This usage of drama was through a story, but demonstrations and narrative can also attract audience attention and brand recall. However, care must be taken not to offend, as was almost certainly the case when the narrator for a 1998 drug television commercial said 'Attention impotent men. All 20 million of you!' This example could easily come under the next heading: shock.

Shock

Shock tactics can also be powerful influencers, but the dividing line between positive and negative response can be thin. Some non-profit organizations use shots of starving children and distressed, abused animals to boost their position, but these tactics can turn as many people off as they turn others on. Benetton has created both situations bringing both praise and criticism for its United Colors of Benetton advertisements. One of its advertisements, for instance, showed a picture of three identical human hearts labelled White, Black, and Yellow. Pre-testing of advertisements becomes particularly important when using this means of arousing emotion.

Fear

Closely related to the above is the use of fear. Volvo has used pictures of people who were involved in horrible car accidents, but who lived because of the car safety features. The Volvo 'Saved My Life' Club helped the company to establish its position of having the safest car, a position it still owns today.

Humour

Humour can be a double-edged sword. Ethnic and minority jokes can offend, even though the majority may enjoy them. Care again has to be taken to make sure that the surprise element of the humour is not followed by pain but by pleasure. Humour used well relaxes audiences and reduces resistance to key messages. The 'moustache' advertisements used to promote milk, which feature well-known personalities like Pete Sampras with a white upper lip, were said to be very effective. San Miguel beer, in one of its advertisements, shows young successful executives enjoying themselves at the end of a working day when suddenly their ties undo themselves and fly away accompanied by the caption 'It's how friends UNWIND'. Joe Boxer's whole brand strategy is based on humour according to the company's founder and Chief Underpants Officer, Nick Graham, who says that 'a true brand should be able to encompass any social structure and income level. We do that with humor. The brand is the amusement park, the products are the souvenirs.' Humour does make viewers more comfortable, if done well.

Warmth

Warmth also relaxes audiences and creates positive mental attitudes. Pictures that project love, patriotism, friendship, caring, and other positive behaviours can be of great assistance to positioning. Johnson and Johnson advertisements for baby and other products have built an amazingly powerful and unassailable positioning of gentleness, care, and love, which is represented in the company's global market share. Even sporting events like the PGA Tour introduce warmth into their advertisements with golfing celebrities such as Nick Price describing, with the help of emotion-building shots, how they have helped many underprivileged people. The commercials end with the tag line 'Anything's Possible'.

Aspiration

Aspirational positioning is a great motivator. Nike's 'Just Do It' campaign is all about self-improvement and success, and advertisements featuring young successful sports persons such as Tiger Woods help reinforce the position. Aspiration as a means of bringing out peoples' emotions is often executed in advertisements with the use of personalities and children.

Music

Music is frequently used in advertisements on television and radio, sometimes via jingles, or as background. It can help recall if memorable, but can also be a source of irritation. Up to 50 per cent of all advertisements use music in a variety of ways, sometimes to arouse sentimentality, as done so successfully with the Hovis bread usage of a North of England brass band, and sometimes to illustrate fun, excitement, seriousness, and other emotions which fit in with the desired positioning and perception. Music is liked across every possible segment and can be used to stimulate emotions in all age groups, but it is particularly appropriate for younger audiences.

Sex

Sexual allure has been used frequently to build in attraction and emotion to positioning, but caution has to be exercised again. There are no adequate guidelines here, but research indicates that sex images should be linked clearly to the product benefits. They are received better by consumers if these are linked also to humour and respect and if the subject is used tastefully. Care should be taken when entering new markets, especially where cultural differences exist. For example, the use of sex in emotional advertising would be problematic in Muslim countries. In Asia, Guinness is combining sex with humour in its advertisements. It has successfully done so in a way that does not offend the different cultural sensibilities.

DIRECT MARKETING

Direct marketing is where consumers deal directly with manufacturers or suppliers in buying items with no intermediary such as a retailer involved. Techniques used here include:
- Direct mail
- Telephone selling
- Press, television, and radio advertising

To be effective it has to be clearly targeted or else it can damage image through unwanted solicitation, as with 'junk' mail. If done well, it can be highly effective not just in sales terms but in building a strong position. The specific advantages are:
- It is effective in targeting well-defined segments.
- It can be good in building relationships over time.
- It contains an interactive quality, thus giving the consumer involvement.
- It is easily measurable in terms of responses.
- It is easily customized to provide specific messages to specific people.

What is absolutely crucial for positioning and image building is that the personality and identity of the company is visible and consistent, and that the correct values are projected. Dell Computers has built its entire brand identity and position through this means, establishing a first-rate image with low-cost, high quality products, and speed of delivery.

SALES PROMOTION

While advertising tends to occupy a large part of the communications budget for many companies, especially those involved in consumer goods, sales promotion techniques are often used to get new products off the ground and establish

positions, to acquire new and lost customers, or to speed up the buying process. Included in sales promotion techniques are:
- Free gifts with purchases
- Redemption coupons
- Contests
- Samples
- Price reductions
- Discount coupons
- Self-liquidating premiums
- Buy 1–get 1 free
- Gift packs
- Privilege cards

The danger with sales promotion activities has usually to do with the possibility that they might weaken a strong position. Powerful positions depend on good perceptions so much that having promotional activities for prestige products, for instance, might damage their image if promotions change consumer perceptions and make them look cheap. Also, long-term promotional campaigns will be costly in terms of support advertising, and consumers may be disappointed when they cease. Some experts have said that they should not be used for brand building for these reasons, but companies like American Express, Citibank, Carlsberg, and others have found them to be useful in increasing their customer base (mainly by getting people to switch brands), increasing individual customer spending, and speeding up the purchase decision. As a general rule, it is better to avoid the price discount type of promotion, and go for the added value type. Adding more value to products rather than subtracting from the price gives consumers good perceptions about value without losing quality perceptions.

Sales promotions are liked by retailers and salespersons for obvious reasons, and can provide a company with a short-term competitive advantage, but there is always the tendency for the competitors to wade in with their own, in which case the results may be short-lived.

PUBLIC RELATIONS

Public relations is often regarded as the 'Cinderella' of positioning. While advertising and sales promotions are very visible and tend to get the spotlight, public relations is often

the unsung hero, achieving a great deal of perception change and management with very little recognition for the role it can play. The basis of public relations is communicating and developing relationships with various target audiences, including:
- Media
- Employees
- Shareholders
- Business partners
- Industry analysts
- Local and foreign investors
- Governments
- The general public
- Customers

This communication can be delivered through press releases, press conferences and interviews, advertorials, newspaper/magazine columns, receptions, sponsorships, and other events.

Public relations often uses mass media but unlike advertising it does not pay for the space, a fact which might be of great appeal to the thrifty. However, it is no easy task and involves a lot of time invested in meeting with these target public, talking with them and persuading them to listen to a certain point of view, and adopting particular attitudes towards a variety of situations and circumstances. It also involves managing to get people, journalists in particular, to report or say favourable things about the client when many competitors are also seeking comment, especially at times of great importance such as new product launches. Public relations is an ongoing process as opposed to a one-off campaign, and the relationships it builds can be of immeasurable benefit in times of crisis. As such, it can be a valuable part of the total communications mix, and must be built in to any positioning communications strategy.

Most large companies have corporate communications departments, whose task, among others, is to look after public relations. Some companies and individuals hire agencies to do it for them, either on retainer basis or for particular projects, or at times of crisis. Some points to note which have relevance for positioning include:

1 Press releases. Most press releases never see the light of day in the media, and should be used sparingly. Inundating journalists with them is not going to get results. They look for really newsworthy items, so routine releases are usually

despatched straight to the waste paper bin. Send press releases only when there is something significant to say that consumers will want to hear about. Remember that the media is only interested in stories that sell—those with a human interest angle.
2 Treating journalists as strategic partners in your business. Relationships are very important, and good relationships are only earned over time. Buying the odd lunch will not buy you media space. Listening to their views is more important because they are the ones who are constantly in touch with the public, and know what the public wants to read, see, or listen to. Also, do not try to be everyone's friend. Choose carefully those few journalists that you believe will, in the long run, be the best choice for your strategy and future situation, and be prepared to invest a lot of time in talking to them.
3 Making the best of opportunities that present themselves. An important development in the industry can give you the chance to comment and push out your name. One bank positioned itself as the 'knowledgeable bank' and managed to get a regular column in an influential newspaper, where it wrote on a frequent basis about financial developments affecting people around the world.
4 Ensuring that events planned to boost the image of the company or its brand(s) are a good 'fit' with the positioning strategy. The same applies to sponsorships. They have to be appropriate to, and in character with, the personality or identity to be projected. When Mattel organized the Barbie Doll World Summit event for charitable purposes, it brought together children from over twenty-seven countries, an event that was totally in line with the company's personality and positioning strategy. When Rolex sponsors sporting events, it only chooses those top tournaments that reinforce the status and prestige of the brand name. And, of course, with both these examples, they are certain of getting the right media coverage targeted at the right audiences.

The Role of Public Relations in Crisis Management

One area where public relations really comes into its own is when crises occur. Public relations specialists are skilled in handling awkward and potentially image-damaging situations, and some are capable of turning a crisis into an opportunity.

The problem with a crisis is that you do not know when it is going to materialize. Nevertheless, many companies are wise enough to develop crisis management manuals that try to anticipate every disaster situation, and prescribe what the response should be. But however good these are, there will always be the unexpected happening.

The speed and type of response is critical to maintaining the image. For instance, in the famous case of Tylenol, Johnson and Johnson's leading analgesic brand, the speed of its withdrawal from the market after poison was found in some of the products probably staved off a catastrophe. The action also demonstrated how concerned the company was about public safety. Its re-entry into the market with tamper-proof packaging reinforced this crucial attribute. In the case of Intel, it did not respond quickly enough when their Pentium crisis happened. The company suffered some damage to its image before eventually recovering from the situation.

The main issue with crisis management is whether or not the crisis should be denied, and many companies opt to deny that there is a crisis until either they work out their response or things get so much worse that they have to admit it. This is the best possible way to destroy the image that has been created, and all the valuable work that has gone into developing a powerful position. Generally, the advice is not to deny it, even if you think it is not really significant. You are dealing with human perceptions, and if people think there is a crisis then there is one, especially if those people are from the media. Perception is reality.

The most skilled people at dealing with such eventualities are the specialized public relations firms, and it is for this reason alone that many organizations place these firms on a monthly retainer basis.

SPONSORSHIPS

Sponsorships can be an extremely effective way of adding more power to positioning, which is why many of the world class companies get involved in them. Sponsorships can involve events (sports, concerts, arts festivals, conferences, and others), organizations (charities, theatres, and others), and the media (TV programmes, magazines, and the like). The advantages are:

- They can give huge exposure to national, regional, and global audiences, especially when they are famous events such as the Olympic Games, Football World Cup, and others.
- They can express the personality of the company or brand by associating it with a particular lifestyle or interest, as seen with Volvo and golf, Rolex and tennis, Cartier and polo, Citibank and leadership.
- They provide spin-off opportunities for advertising and public relations at the events themselves and in the media coverage.
- They can influence the emotions of the viewing public who often will want to associate themselves with the event by doing so with the company or the brand.
- They can create awareness among, and influence, other target audiences including distributors, government, and media.

The disadvantages come mainly from two sources:

- Sponsorships on any major scale are costly, and this is extended beyond the actual sponsor as in general a similar amount of money needs to be spent to promote the company association.
- They can damage the image if the sponsorship does not fit with the positioning.

As with all communications and image-building activities, the need to understand the customer is paramount, and whatever is the subject of sponsorship it must hold the same values and associations as the sponsoring organization. Tag Heuer is a good example of appropriate sponsorship. It is positioned as a prestige sports watch and is the official timekeeper of the 1999 FIA Formula One World Championship.

TOTALLY CONSISTENT AND APPROPRIATE ACTIVITIES IN STRATEGIC POSITIONING

Whatever strategies are used, consistency is the key to success in positioning. Within a total communications campaign, the same values and messages should be clearly identified in every activity, be it advertising, sponsorships, or other methods used. Everything presented to consumers should be appropriate to the positioning. For instance, if the positioning for a product is designed to build a more prestigious image, then any promotional premiums or incentives given away should also reflect that desired image. Cheap give-aways would undermine the position. Similarly, any advertising commercials should use only shots of places, people, and products which fit with the position you are trying to develop in people's minds. All communications should be carefully planned with this in mind.

TAG LINES IN POSITIONING

Be careful not to confuse tag lines with positioning statements. Tag lines are used in advertising, on corporate signage, packaging, and other aspects of communication. Their main purpose is to synthesize the total positioning, and to offer a promise to the target audience. They do not work in isolation, always being prefaced by some form of communication. They do not, indeed cannot, say everything. Rather, they have to be broad—able to 'lock down' a host of different messages, the thrust of which may change over time. They should, however, impart a sense of direction and provide the ultimate 'full stop'—representing the final impression and ideally, a call to action, conveyed to the viewer, listener, or reader.

The challenge in developing tag lines is that they should firmly present the 'difference', claim superiority, effectively cover off personality, service, technological sophistication, or other important messages, cope with change, and be equally relevant to various markets. Most of all, they have to convey a sense of promise, excitement and experience, all in three to four words!

Tag lines are often developed with little thought to all of these considerations, and to what impact they might have on customer relationships. Worse still, they are sometimes created in the absence of any positioning statement, and with total disregard for the capabilities of the company. An example of this might be a company that has the tag line 'Dedicated to Customer Service' but which provides a poor level of service. To retain and attract customers, many others in existence offer platitudes and promises which, however, cannot be delivered. The result of poorly thought-out tag lines can be a tremendous loss of consumer confidence and corporate credibility.

If we take airlines as examples, tag lines range from the straightforward (Garuda—The Airline of Indonesia), to the stolid (KLM—The Reliable Airline), to the gushy (Air Lanka—It's a Taste of Paradise), to the almost unbelievable (China Airlines—Always from the Heart from Us to You). Some companies use them as part of their differentiation strategy, but when viewed without their powerful advertising they appear to be very similar, for instance, Four Seasons Hotels and Resorts (Defining the art of service at 40 hotels in 19 countries) and Swissotel (A passion for perfection). The better ones are simple yet evocative, such as Singapore Airlines—A Great Way to Fly. Singapore Airlines is typical of companies that take tag lines seriously, and to live up to the promise it continually works on product and service improvements, currently investing heavily in both while competitors are cutting back on expenditure and reducing costs.

In some cases, tag lines are changed over time, as products and markets evolve. Some companies change them quite frequently in the absence of such changes. However, frequent changes are not desirable as they cause customer confusion and waste residual value of communications efforts. Usually tag line changes indicate a lack of solid direction or management confidence in an organization's marketing activities. It is worthwhile giving a lot of thought to the creation of a tag line, and to end up with one that not only summarizes the positioning, but is also based on reality.

Employing Agencies or Doing it Yourself

The question always arises of whether positioning and its execution should be determined internally or by outside agencies. The answer is that both should be involved, even though conflicts will inevitably occur. Beginning with *research*, the first important issue that should be dealt with before any agency is considered is that of what research specifically needs to be done, as the variety of data that can be collected is enormous. As far as positioning is concerned, some of the questions that might need answering if not already investigated are:
- Who are our customers?
- Who are the 20 per cent of our customers accounting for 80 per cent of our business?

- What are their profiles?
- Do we know what they really need and want?
- Where and how can they be reached?
- How do they perceive us, our products, and our services?
- How does our image compare with those of competitors?
- Why do people like us? What attracts them to us?
- What do they like about our personality?
- How would they like to see us improve?
- Why are the loyal customers loyal?
- Why have customers left us and switched to other brands?
- Who are the marginal people who might or might not stay with our competitors or us?
- What are the competitors doing to alter the perceptions of people about themselves and us?
- What do we know already about these items of information?
- Do we need to develop perceptual maps to help us read the minds of consumers?
- What more do we need to know to be able to strengthen our position?

Many of these questions can be answered by setting in motion internal research—by analysing data already available and by asking customers. The quality of the internal surveys will depend to some extent on the adequacy of the customer database, and whether the technology exists inside the company to manipulate and interrogate that data.

Outside research agencies are to be selected with care. They often possess sophisticated software modelling tools, but these do not fit all occasions and requirements although some agencies would try to make out that they do. If an outside agency is to be selected, it is crucial that a thorough brief is given stating exactly what the strategic positioning issue is, and what precise information is required for decision-making purposes. Often this might require a small amount of outside consultancy advice. Many consultants end up being called in for larger amounts of time to either rebrief the agency, or try to make out what the data is actually saying. The right questions must be asked. One area where research agencies themselves are found to be weak is in the *strategic* interpretation of data collected. If the right questions have been asked, they can explain what the data means now, but they lack the skills of the strategist in determining what courses of action might be taken, with what results, and which is most salient to the strategic problem facing the organization.

With *advertising and promotion*, there are some similarities and differences to be found. Advertising and promotion is not quite the same as research in that it is virtually impossible not to get an agency involved. But again care must be taken as the quality of agency work is extremely variable, and mistakes can be very costly, not just in terms of money but image also.

POINTS TO CONSIDER

Advertising can create very powerful positioning, but before getting to the agency brief there are four important things to consider.

First, it is normal to have several agencies to 'pitch' for the business, and for the best one to be selected. Agencies will always wheel out their top team for this occasion, promising that what you see is what you get when they work on your account. Do not be fooled here. It is rare for this to happen, and a lot of ill feeling and misunderstandings can arise when the work is delegated to relatively junior staff who have neither the experience nor the knowledge to give advice on strategic positioning. As part of the contract it is advisable to have the team members specified, together with what roles they will play, and on what occasions they will attend meetings.

Secondly, it has traditionally been the case that only one agency tends to be selected, even by the global companies. However, there appears to be a polarization among agencies, with the large integrated ones that claim to offer everything you can possibly want at one end, and smaller more specialized agencies, who look after specific areas like direct marketing, at the other. Some of the latter are subsidiaries of the former but totally self-sufficient. There are no hard and fast rules as to which you should choose, but with positioning in mind the strategic ability must be evident. The trend in selection, leaving aside global companies that often choose one global agency for consistency of execution, is for companies to work with smaller agencies that can offer speed and flexibility, but do make sure they are competent in all areas necessary.

A final word of caution is to make sure that the creative side of the agency is good, as evidenced by the ability of its people to listen to and articulate the problem, its track record in awards, and so on. The relationship with the agency's creative team is often the one that is subject to most pressure, as creative staff tend to defend their favourite ideas very strongly, even if the client feels that they do not fit well with the strategy. Also, an agency that is creative now may lose its edge over time especially if the creative director leaves. Review several agencies regularly to see which one has the best creative ideas. Some companies appoint a panel of agencies and give assignments to the one that is the best at that particular time.

THE AGENCY BRIEF

The success of advertising depends largely on the effectiveness of the brief. If you do not give the agency a clear strategic brief, you will inevitably be disappointed with their ideas, and there will be a lot of heated debate about what it is that you are actually trying to say to the target audience(s). This will waste time and money for both parties and even strain the relationship. The critical elements here are to give the agency

- Relevant, well-written positioning statement(s) for each product or brand. A full verbal discussion should take place with the entire agency account team on these documents, so that an understanding of the desired position and the important aspects of differentiation are in no doubt.
- A personality statement, outlining the human side of the company or product to be positioned.
- A statement of the strategic objectives and results expected, in terms of as many criteria as possible, including market share, sales units, and/or turnover, customer satisfaction index, or other appropriate image and brand equity measurements.
- Any previous research *information* or documentation such as tracking studies, perceptual maps, competitor strategy, analysis, and others.

Case Study

SINGAPORE TELECOM (SINGTEL IDD 001): CREATIVE, INTEGRATED, AND CUSTOMER-FOCUSED COMMUNICATIONS

Occasionally companies have to change consumer mind associations as fast as possible, and add to positional strength at the same time. This is not easy to do with a product that is not really exciting, and therein lies the challenge. Singapore Telecom (SingTel) had to face such a challenge when changing their IDD number in a way that would not alienate the customer base, and which would have rapid results. Clear and effective communications was clearly needed. The advertising brief, execution, and results are briefly described below.

Advertising Brief

1 To provide a visual icon that is memorable and instantly recognized as the branding device for SingTel IDD 001, which is the new access code for IDD. Previously the access code was 005.
2 The icon device must be contemporary with an 'international feel' to reflect the personality of IDD users who are well travelled and have friends and family overseas. The association of the icon must be seamlessly interwoven with the access code for international direct dial which is 001. This is to aid awareness and easy recall when people need to call overseas.
3 The value proposition of 001 to be communicated included: (a) network clarity; (b) instant connections to any of 200 plus countries; and (c) competitive rates.

Target Audience

The main target audience was people aged 18–50 with a monthly income of S$3000–S$5000. Being a branding campaign to lodge in the mind of consumers the new access code for IDD and to assist the effective building of a brand personality for 001, national media were used.

Advertising Execution

The ad was meant to spoof the 007 spy character and change the tag line from 007 'Licence to Kill' to 001 'Licence to Call'. A James Bond look-alike actor was used. The timing was excellent because it coincided with the movie release of the Bond film 'Tomorrow Never Dies'. It was topical, interesting, and instantly connected with the viewers while riding on the crest of publicity generated by the new movie release. 001— the man with the handphone was thus conceived. Branding properties included the black-and-white circle devices, gun barrels, graphics, and others, with music scored to complement the mood and tone of the 001 personality. Three versions of the campaign to communicate the key values proposition as outlined above were executed. A combination of TV, print, direct mail, and outdoor media were used.

Research Findings: Post Campaign

SingTel always measures its marketing communications to see how effective they have been, and how their positioning has been affected. In this case the results were as follows:

- The advertising campaign had a high level of awareness— 98 per cent (the percentage of people that had seen, heard, or read about it).
- Six in ten of the respondents found the advertisements interesting.
- The association of IDD 001 with 007 made the code easier to remember.
- The sponsorship of the James Bond movies on Friday nights reinforced the recall level for 001 ad campaign.
- The consistency of the 001 'look and feel' made it easy to relate to 001 despite the three advertisement executions
- It was found that the highest and most positive responses were from high value users. Looking after these people is always important for any company.

The whole campaign was customer focused. At all times, when cheaper, less creative communications could have been used, SingTel invested in creative ways of communicating the key message designed to make things easier for the customer. This undoubtedly enhanced the corporate image, as well as achieving the product objective.

(*Source*: Singapore Telecom Corporate Marketing)

Positioning and the Search for Success

As positioning actually occurs in people's minds, it is very important to try to gain a clear understanding of what their thoughts are, in other words how your target audience(s) sees your company, product, service, in comparison to your competitors. If the target audience is small you can, of course, simply ask them. If it is larger you can use sampling techniques to assess their views, as is the case with polling techniques such as those carried out by Mori or Gallup, and quantitative techniques used by many research agencies. However, there are other methods that can be used, and for positioning purposes, two of the most interesting and rewarding are focus groups and perceptual mapping. Because positioning success depends on establishing a powerful position based on what people like and want, focus group and perceptual mapping research are particularly appropriate to both positioning strategy and evaluation. These two methodologies are described here followed by an example of how you can use them together for positioning purposes.

Perceptual Mapping

Perceptual mapping is one of the most useful techniques for giving a pictorial view of how something is positioned in relation to competitors. There are simple and relatively complex techniques available for creating perceptual maps, but the output always gives a useful insight into how people perceive the subjects of the study and their images. Normally, these maps are outputs of data analysis that plot the different perceptions on two dimensions. Products can be compared on attributes such as price, quality, and others. Companies can see what consumers think about their personality characteristics, and their products or services. For instance, several airlines could be rated against each other on the dimensions of friendly/unfriendly in-flight service and ground handling efficiency/inefficiency. There is virtually no limit to what aspects of competitive comparison can be explored using this technique, as with the beer illustration given here and, for example, with hair shampoos which can also have several different attributes of interest to various consumers.

There are two ways of proceeding with perceptual mapping. First, based on definitive knowledge of what is important to the people you are interested in, the relevant dimensions can be chosen and responses obtained to rate the objects against each other by the relatively simple process of asking for rankings via rating scales. Varied analyses would then be used to interpret the data for assessment. In the absence of knowledge regarding what elements are important to people, the dimensions can be derived from responses about certain attributes or qualities which reveal what preferences, similarities, and differences are perceived by the population sample. This procedure is normally carried out using a technique called multidimensional scaling, which can be used to measure:
- Similarities or differences between items
- Consumer preferences between items
- Consumers' brand attribute ratings

Responses using either method can be represented in different graphical ways, such as concentric circles, grids, or hierarchies. The technique can also be adapted for group meetings where members place tabs or marks on a 'map' of the attributes or qualities under discussion and discuss their reasoning. In this way numerous brands, for example, can be sorted quickly, and valuable feedback gained on product/service features, attributes, packaging, image, and other areas of interest.

Additional advantages of perceptual mapping are:
- A great deal can be learned about the strengths and weaknesses of you and your competitors.
- The maps help clarify perceptual differences between different target audiences, thereby giving you a means of segmenting a market. If produced regularly over time, perceptual changes (which are normally slow to evolve) can be revealed.
- The information is easily presentable and understandable in the map format.
- The maps can help you decide on which strategic positioning alternatives to pursue, and strategic opportunities for improving your image and market situation.

This last point is particularly important because first, the map spaces show how far away or how near you are to your preferred position, and what needs to be done to get there. Secondly, they show the relative closeness of your own and competitors' image or products in people's minds. This can help you decide whether you want to move your position, either to be closer to the customer than them if there is a suitable space, or to move away from them if they are too close to you. Thirdly, they might lead you to a decision to introduce a totally new product or a brand extension if there are consumer needs that remain unsatisfied with current offerings from yourself or the competitors.

The two limitations of perceptual mapping are that first, all dimensions of concern to consumers cannot be looked at on one map. Nevertheless, having more than one map representing different areas of concern is not a big problem, and there are now techniques available that produce three or more dimensional maps. Secondly, as small numbers of people are involved compared to quantitative measures, and wide ranging discussions ensue, it is sometimes difficult to generalize and predict behaviour for large audiences. But the more tightly defined the market segment under investigation is, the more effective the methodology becomes. Nevertheless, the insights gained from perceptual mapping are very good for looking at the positioning of existing and new products. Because of the advantages, perceptual mapping remains probably the most widely used method of tracking how a company or a product's personality and image fare against the competition.

Focus Groups

Focus groups are becoming more popular as part of a general trend to concentrate more on qualitative research methodology as opposed to gathering quantitative data. Quantitative research usually tries to quantify such items as share, size, growth, and demographics of a specific market, while qualitative research deals with the question of why something is happening. The reason for the trend in qualitative research is the need to understand how people's minds work, by exploring below-the-surface attitudes and feelings about companies, products, services, or people. A typical focus group will consist of six to ten people selected to discuss a topic or

topics, and a skilled moderator, who uses a set of questions to trigger discussion points, and normally records the session on video or tape. It is very important that the composition of the groups is correct in terms of the precise market segments that must be covered, otherwise the data retrieved might be meaningless. Careful consideration must therefore be given to demographic and psychographic group composition. Segmentation options and techniques have been discussed in more detail in Chapter 6. Investigative questions might be included in areas such as:
- Product recall and awareness
- Consumption patterns—amounts, frequency, location, and others
- Brand preferences
- Saliency of company/product/service attributes (for example, features, price, taste, effectiveness, packaging, ease of use)

Typical questions for discussion might be:
- What brand do you prefer and in what situations?
- What is important to you in choosing a particular product?
- Have you changed brands in the past? When and why?
- What words would you use to describe the following brands?
- If you were to describe this company as a person which words would you choose?

In trying to understand the rationale for why people associate themselves with specific items, questions and discussion will often concentrate on image perceptions, for instance, finding out what personality characteristics they attach to different brands, and exploring the similarities and differences they think are important. The reason for this kind of investigative framework is to link up the self-image of the target audience with the perceived image of what they prefer to buy, because people often buy things that match their own self-image, or one to which they aspire.

The following simplified example illustrates the difference between the qualitative and quantitative approaches. If you are involved in the market for a particular beverage, say beer, in a particular country, or region of a country, quantitative research might be used to find out what the total size of the market for that product is, and how fast it is growing. More specifically, it might be used to establish what market share each competitor has in particular market segments, and how these relative market shares are changing over time. The segments could relate to different products, and to the types of people who buy those products. For instance, you might discover that you are losing share to other competitors in the market where your bottled lager product competes, particularly in a higher-income, lower-age group of 28–35-year-old people who are urban dwellers and social drinkers. However, you do not know why this is happening even though you have found out which brand is gaining share at our expense. To get the answer to this question you would need to carry out some more specific quantitative and some qualitative research, which would include focus groups, containing people who typically represent this target segment, who buy your product and those of other competitors, including the one that is gaining share.

COMBINING QUANTITATIVE AND QUALITATIVE RESEARCH FOR STRATEGIC POSITIONING

The example described below shows how both types of research can be used together to assess current perceptions of product, brand, or any image, together with options for future improvement.

Step One: The first stage in assessing your positioning *vis-à-vis* the selected competitors is to get target consumers to fill out a questionnaire that asks them to compare each brand or competitor with every other brand in terms of what, in their minds, makes them similar or different.

Step Two: Each person is then asked to complete a short questionnaire comprising of rating scales comparing various attributes of the range of brands (products or companies) of interest. This might be a predetermined list of attributes, plus others that people have said are of importance during the first step, and would provide some objective quantitative data about how they compare the brands concerned (in this case beer) on criteria such as:
- Price
- Taste
- Packaging

158 ◻ STRATEGIC POSITIONING

- Strength
- Image
- Availability
- Effect
- Name
- Colour

And/or any other possible purchasing influences. These two steps will help you map the relative positions of the various brands within a 'perceptual space' defined by the consumers themselves.

Step Three: The Focus Group Discussions. Within the focus groups, more probing and open-ended questions would be asked to find out through group discussion why they prefer certain brands to others, on what occasions, how they would describe a brand X or a brand Y drinker, and even how they would describe the brands themselves as if they were people. It would also be of interest to find out if they have changed brands at all, and why. These questions would give you ideas about how you could reposition your product to gain greater appeal with this kind of consumer.

The output of the whole process would be a series of perceptual maps which plot and illustrate the minds of the target customer group, revealing how they place one brand in relation to others on the various dimensions, and a wealth of qualitative information used by consumers themselves to describe their decision-making behaviour.

Figure 8.1 shows what one typical perceptual map might look like, together with interpretive information.

This example shows one of a series of hypothetical maps produced for the beer market study. Initially, the two axes would have no names attached to them, and the brands would have appeared as dots in the various spaces of the map representing how close or how far away from each other they are. At this stage the creative powers of the researcher come to the fore. He examines the brands in the product space, noting the distances between each as they relate to the two dimensions, and from this will attempt to give the two dimensions a name which best describes what is discriminating between each. For example, in the figure, the researcher has named each of the two dimensions, according to his subjective interpretation, as modernity and prestige. He reached these con-

FIGURE 8.1
Example of a Perceptual Map

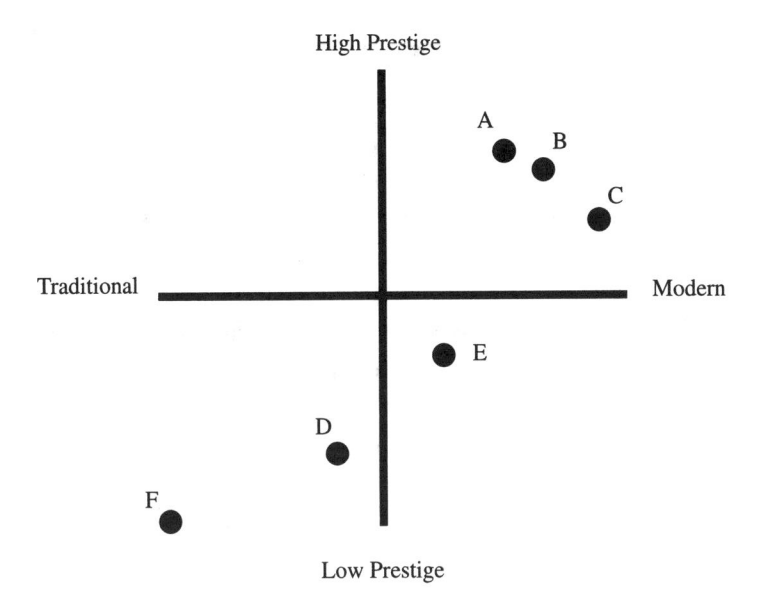

Perceptual map with axes High Prestige/Low Prestige (vertical) and Traditional/Modern (horizontal). Brands A, B, C are in the upper-right (High Prestige, Modern) quadrant, with A highest and C furthest right. Brand E sits just below the horizontal axis near center. Brand D is in the lower-right region near the vertical axis. Brand F is in the lower-left (Traditional, Low Prestige) quadrant.

clusions from a combination of his knowledge of existing brands and the perceptual distances between them as depicted in the perceptual map. Therefore the figure maps each brand in two-dimensional space defined by the two brand attributes of:

- How prestigiously the brands are perceived
- How traditional or modern they are seen to be

Some researchers, given this situation in the beer market, use regression techniques to map dimensions of known product attributes, such as price, strength, and (bitter/smooth) taste, over the figure as an aid in interpreting the unnamed dimensions that are really discriminating between the brands. Figure 8.2 shows such a situation. For instance, the known product attribute of price lies close to the perpendicular axis suggesting that this dimension is strongly related to prestige. This gives the researcher an extra clue on what to name the axis.

In this instance, Brand A is seen to be the most prestigious, followed by Brands B and C, while Brand F has the least prestigious image.

Brand C is perceived as being the most modern, and Brand F

160 ❏ STRATEGIC POSITIONING

FIGURE 8.2
Perceptual Map with a Price Attribute Overlay
Using Regression Techniques

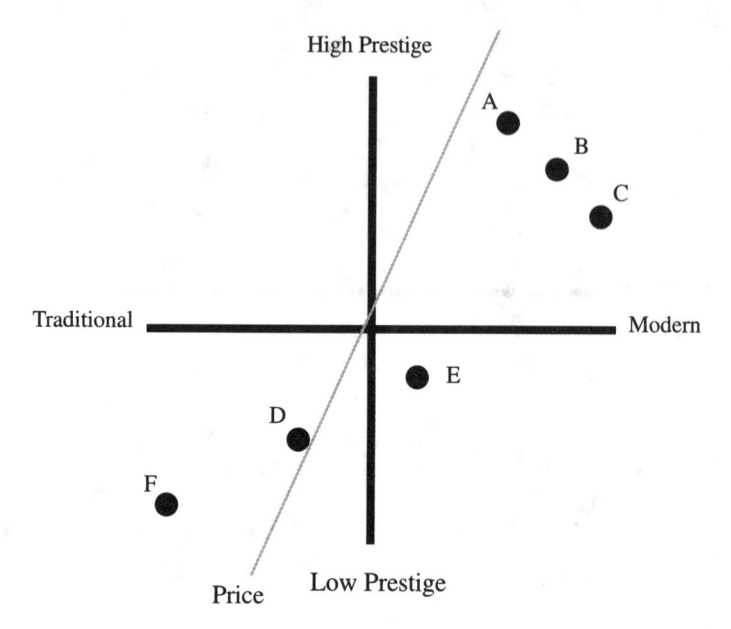

as the most traditional, followed by Brand D. Brand E is close to the centre of the map, suggesting no strong associations with either dimension in consumer minds.

The various strategic options available for these brands might be:

1 If these two dimensions were revealed by the analysis as being of greatest importance to consumers, which they might well be in the high end premium section of the market, then Brands A and B are perceived as being very close, with hardly any differentiation. In beer markets, this type of position would be typical of that held by global foreign brands such as Heineken. The opportunity here would be for either A or B to try to become even stronger in this quadrant by moving out towards the top right of the map. This could possibly be achieved by further increasing price, and reinforcing the elements of prestige and status with exclusive, sophisticated brand imagery in advertisements.

2 Brand C also has that opportunity, but would have to reposition itself by concentrating more on changing consumer perceptions about its ability to represent prestige

and status. This repositioning exercise would draw on focus group information as to what consumers believe the combination of prestige and modernity does for them, and how they use the brands to demonstrate this.

3 At face value on this map, Brand F has little chance in the upper market, but could do well with consumers who are not so bothered about status, but value heritage. If this was a national as opposed to a foreign brand, then strengthening this position could bring good results with a more blue-collar segment. Consequently, advertising and promotional activity appealing to the elements of patriotism and value for money would underpin the positioning strategy.

4 Brand E has the problem of appealing to many customer types but in a limited way. It cannot compete at the high end, but has a chance perhaps of repositioning to capture the quadrant where prestige might not be a buying factor, but where modernity is. This might be the case with a younger age group, and would have to be tested out with such a segment.

5 As far as any prospective new products are concerned, there would appear to be a major opportunity in the top left quadrant, where a combination of prestige and tradition could create a powerful position, maybe with older, nationalistic consumers. Testing out this potential positioning could bring substantial future success if the market exists and is large enough to warrant the investment.

Once these dimensions have been defined, they can be validated by further testing and confirmatory studies using other samples and focus groups.

PREFERENCE MAPPING

The perceptual mapping process described above could be taken one stage further by identifying what the 'ideal' position or preference for the consumer would be by using additional techniques which involve rating the attributes of products in the study. The research could also take into account the weighted importance of each attribute, and produce clusters of responses that represent differences between consumer groups or segments. Taking the same attributes as those in the two preceding figures, two different clusters might show up as follows:

FIGURE 8.3
A Consumer Preference Map

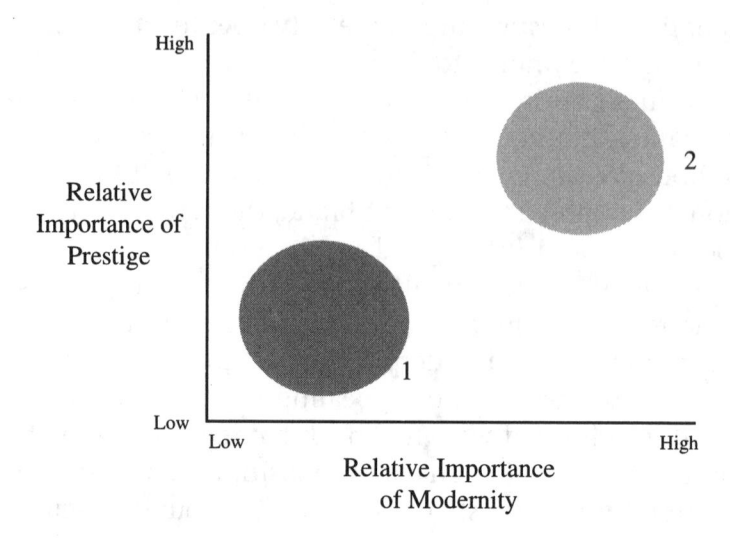

In this case, two segments of the respondents clearly have two different ideal points shown as clusters. Cluster 1 prefers the traditional and less prestigious brands while Cluster 2 seeks the more modern prestigious ones.

This is called preference mapping, and it results in a perceptual map which can be overlaid on other perceptual maps to reveal the consumers' preferred position and indicating the spaces between products. Preference mapping provides even more information to help strategic positioning decision-making, and can be particularly beneficial when a company is considering how to launch a new product.

ONE-TO-ONE (DEPTH) INTERVIEWS

This type of evaluation is obviously more costly than interviewing groups of people, and the numbers covered in a depth interview survey are usually restricted because of this. It is normally used when it is difficult to get detailed information, and as the word 'depth' implies, the aim is to get a thorough insight into what are peoples' thoughts, attitudes, needs, wants, and motives. This methodology has its strength in that people are normally interviewed in the locations where they interact with or purchase the product or service. So in the beer example given, they would be interviewed in locations where people representative of the specific target segment were drinking beer, perhaps a restaurant or hotel bar. This has the advantage that the subjects are selected on the basis of what they are really doing and not what they say they do. It can be useful for positioning because it offers the opportunity to explore the reasoning that lies behind the perceptions through the use of follow-up questions and individual discussion. They provide for confidentiality, and are good for subjects that are sensitive in nature, such as feminine hygiene.

Depth interviews require highly skilled interviewers, who have experience in dealing with relatively unstructured questionnaires, and also staff who are capable of strategically interpreting the relatively unstructured data that results. Typical questions that might be asked in a half-hour interview might be:

- Why do you choose to buy that particular brand?
- What other brands would you consider if that one was not available?
- If you had a totally free choice of any product of this type, which would you choose and why?

Data would also be gathered relating to sex, age, consumption patterns, and others.

MORE TECHNIQUES FOR TRACKING POSITIONING SUCCESS

Other ways by which you can track how effective your positioning strategies have been include the following qualitative and quantitative methods, which can be carried out with individuals or focus groups. Many of them are particularly helpful in assessing the success of personality positioning, and so they can be used for branded products and services, companies, nations, places, and individuals. While they would not cover great numbers of people, they can give a very quick guide to image impact with specific target audiences. They are:

- Self-image and attribute matching
- Obituary sketching
- Pictures/Collages
- Recalled experiences
- Difference statements
- What ifs

- Personality descriptions
- Photo sorting
- Chronography
- Analogies and metaphors
- Marriage/partnership choices
- Advertising
- Direct marketing and sales promotion

Self-image and Attribute Matching

Positioning has a great deal to do with people's self-concept and image, and it is interesting to assess the results on the basis of how closely the two are matched. They tend to want to be associated with products and companies that fit with their own self-image, or one to which they aspire or like. They tend not to be attracted to those that do not fit in with this desired image. Positioning and segmentation are inseparable, and the tighter the definition of the consumer profile that is targeted, the easier it is to determine whether the positioning has been effective or not. This type of evaluation is particularly appropriate for positioning based on personality, where the strategy has concentrated on projecting personality traits to which it is thought the audience will be attracted. Questions put to target customer groups ask about their perceptions of personality characteristics of both themselves and the company/brand being evaluated.

The degree of success can be measured on rating scales which can be combined graphically to show a profile of how close the fit is between the self-image of the consumer and the perceived personality of the product or company that is the goal of the positioning activity.

In this hypothetical example, shown in Figure 8.4, there is a reasonably good fit between the consumer group self-concept and the image of Brand A on most characteristics, but the problem appears to be that the brand (be it product or company) is not really seen to be as friendly, exciting, and responsive as the customers feel they are. It may be a cause of falling sales or reduced brand loyalty among this market segment, but if remedied may solve such problems and increase the rate of new customer acquisition. Further inquiry via focus groups would reveal the meaning behind the gaps, and then the company would have some repositioning work to

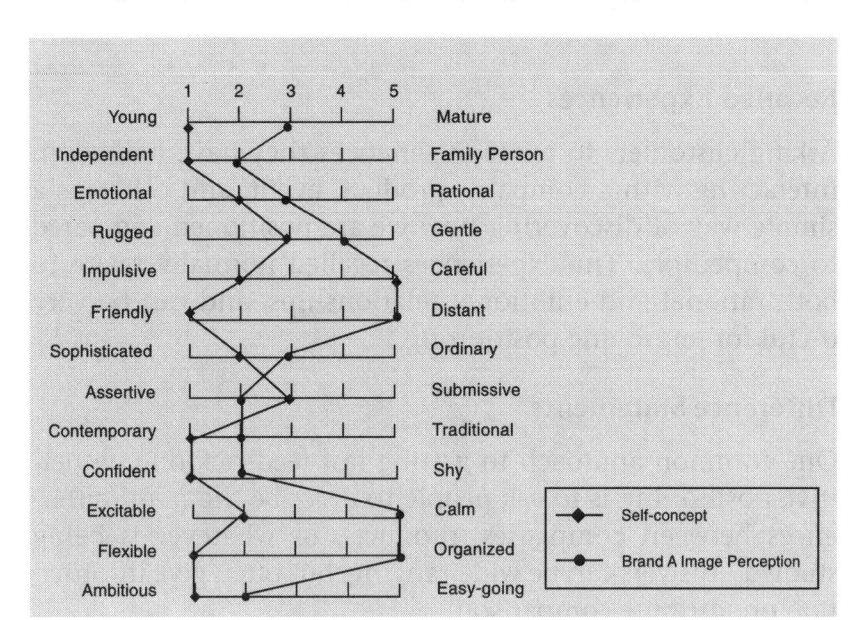

FIGURE 8.4
Example of the Fit between Image and the Self-concept of Consumers

Self-concept pole		Opposite pole
Young		Mature
Independent		Family Person
Emotional		Rational
Rugged		Gentle
Impulsive		Careful
Friendly		Distant
Sophisticated		Ordinary
Assertive		Submissive
Contemporary		Traditional
Confident		Shy
Excitable		Calm
Flexible		Organized
Ambitious		Easy-going

Legend: ♦ Self-concept; ● Brand A Image Perception

do, not just in terms of communicating to that audience that the brand is better on these dimensions than was thought, but possibly through product/service improvements that demonstrate this is the case.

Obituary Sketching

Getting staff and customers to write a short obituary for the company or product together with others for competitors can reveal true feelings about current positioning. Comments such as 'You were never there for me' and 'I always valued your honesty and friendship' are typical, and these, even though valuable insights in themselves, can be pursued in subsequent conversations to establish deeper thoughts and meanings.

Pictures/Collages

Showing individual or collections of pictures or photographs to consumers, or even getting them to draw simple pictures, can be a useful way of revealing the associations they have with companies and products. An alternative process is to ask them to assemble items into their own collage representative of their thoughts. Descriptions of the choices they make orally or in writing about scenes given to them can also contribute to a further understanding of the positions occupied in their minds.

Recalled Experiences

Asking customers to relate experiences they have had when interacting with a company, product, event, and others is a simple way of discovering how we are positioned compared to competitors. The experiences recalled normally relate to both rational and emotional relationships, and can be very useful for improving positioning.

Difference Statements

One common approach to getting fast feedback on competitive positioning is to ask people to describe the main differences between companies, products, or whatever is being studied. Answers can be wide-ranging, but often give information on attribute comparison.

What Ifs

This technique asks people to describe your company or product as if it were an animal, a car, a food, a holiday destination, and so on. Many examples can be used, the aim being to test out the consistency of the position and to understand the reasoning behind the choices. This is a fun exercise and goes down very well with small groups of targeted consumers.

Personality Descriptions

This method is similar to the above but asks people to describe the personality of your product/company compared to that of your competitors by listing the main characteristics or traits they perceive. This is an exercise which is very important and beneficial if the positioning has a personality-based foundation, and is easily accomplished by asking questions such as 'What kind of person do you think company X is?'

Photo Sorting

This is a combination of the picture/collage technique and personality descriptions, and it asks people to sort out photographs or pictures of various types of people and relate these to different products or companies according to their perceptions of them.

Chronography

A more complex methodology is to observe people in their own environment, and to draw conclusions from their behaviour. This can generate insights into positioning and future strategy by looking at how they interact with products/services/companies, or by following their thought processes when making decisions or choices about what to do or buy. It is complex because it involves a lot of behavioural analysis, and the co-operation of representatives of the target audience(s). A bank in the United States found it valuable when it followed the process of how people in a specific age group made their financial decisions by videotaping them in their homes as they discussed financial planning and decision-making.

Analogies and Metaphors

Asking consumers to relate to products, services and companies through the use of analogies, and metaphors can produce interesting information about perceived attributes and characteristics.

Marriage/Partnership Choices

This is another method of finding out about the attributes and personality characteristics of brands and companies, which works by asking people which other products or companies would make the ideal partner. It often results in useful data on the strengths and weaknesses of your brand or company and the competitors. In an informal, fun way, this method discovers what the perceived characteristics are and why people think of your brand or company in the way they do.

Advertising

The success of advertising is somewhat difficult to measure, but there are available techniques for tracking awareness, recall, and attitudes, before and after the advertising takes place. The creative element of advertising is the most influential aspect in terms of attracting or repelling consumers, and endorsing or diluting the corporate or product image. Good creative advertising can make the campaign highly successful, but very often money is wasted on advertising to which consumers are indifferent or indisposed. For this very important reason all creative advertising should be pretested with consumers at several stages before final production stage. Once the advertisements are underway, you need to assess their impact and there are several ways of doing this.

Awareness (in the form of recognition and recall) and attitude measurement for products and brands is sometimes carried out using aided and unaided responses and mentions by consumers. This is not without its problems, as in deciding what the exact definition of the product category is, and in accounting for differences in samples. More sophisticated techniques to measure 'Share of Mind' can also be found to assess visibility and opinions held by people, and these can be tracked over time, but again this is not an exact science, and results should be treated only as indications of positioning impact as opposed to precise evidence of how people are likely to behave. Other measurements can add to such information by segmenting users and looking at their degree of commitment, and by looking at non-users with respect to their degree of availability in terms of switching. Many companies do not bother with these types of studies and wait to see the impact on sales, but sales increases can be a result of other factors, and it is best to test out why they have increased.

A point to note is that advertising agencies are notoriously reluctant to have their work assessed, but if it makes a difference between getting the account or not they will do it. There is a growing trend now to relate the remuneration of advertising agencies to results achieved. However, in measuring the results of their activities it is best to involve an independent research agency, not just for objectivity, but also because they have the most up-to-date techniques. As mentioned in Chapter 5, there is now more pressure on brand managers to measure brand equity in its various forms, which in itself means that advertising agencies will be forced to become more accountable.

Direct Marketing and Sales Promotion

Direct marketing and sales promotion activities are designed primarily as sales vehicles rather than image builders, but any such activities will have an impact on image. The cost benefits of direct marketing and sales promotions are easily calculable, but the impact on image less so, unless it is assumed that sales increases represent an increase in the strength of consumer perceptions, which may not be valid. With surveys, however, it is possible to ascertain whether or not the campaign materials have contributed to the image and positioning. As with advertising, it is highly advisable to pretest any direct marketing or promotional activity in order to maximize results.

MONITORING AND PROTECTING THE POSITION

As mentioned at the very beginning of this book, positioning is strategic and should be treated like any other part of corporate strategy in that it should be accorded a high level of importance, and be pursued with immense determination. Many corporate failures have occurred because this realization is not present; you see it in the apparent inability of companies and managers to maintain consistent and appropriate activities. There are many reasons why actual and potential good positions are destroyed in this way, including:

- New managers wanting to make their mark by trying something different
- Existing managers getting bored and doing the same
- Companies allowing agencies to dominate thinking and moving off strategy
- Frequent changes in top management who do not put positioning as a priority
- A lack of knowledge of the current position and competitive threats
- Inadequate monitoring of company-wide activities which can have an impact on positioning
- A lack of understanding of market dynamics

- Complacency, especially when times are good
- Taking the option of short-term gains at the expense of long-term position building
- Not understanding the evolving needs and wants of consumers, and their changing perceptions

The responsibility rests with top management, and the setting up of a suitable mechanism for protecting and strengthening the positioning strategy would stop these from occurring. Few companies do positioning audits, for instance. But if carried out frequently these would help avoid many positioning failures. Chapter 10 provides a step-by-step question guide to the positioning process which will be helpful to companies wishing to improve the monitoring and measurement of positioning success.

Issues in Strategic Positioning

This chapter focuses on some of the key issues being explored and tackled at present in the field of strategic positioning. Some of you may be grappling with these problems now. Others will be interested in looking at them because they represent challenges and trends that are going to affect all of us in various degrees in the next century. If so, I hope the book and this chapter helps in some way to answer questions you are asking.

THE REPOSITIONING OF NATIONS

There are two main reasons why countries need to concern themselves with 'image'.
1 They wish to attract various customer groups. As with corporations, in the final analysis they are interested in marketing and selling their products, ideas, and services to people in other countries. To succeed in achieving this aim they have to increase their exports and attract a good inflow of foreign investment by appearing to be (in the eyes of potential 'buyers') better than the competitors. And just as companies have found that the best way to do this is not usually via lowest price, but perceived value, so countries are beginning to do so as well. There is a dawning recognition that image is made up of perceived value in consumer minds, and that value can consist of many intangible as opposed to tangible aspects of the customer relationship.
2 There is a need to manage perceptions and control their image. The South-East Asian countries, for instance, are now suffering, almost collectively, from a poor image manifesting itself in the form of a lack of investor confidence. There is a perception gap between what each country wants to be seen as (identity) and how each is seen (image). And every country wants to make sure that there is no perception gap.
So governments are starting to try to make sure that their countries' image matches their identity. Whether they like it or not countries have an image—so it is better for the image to be controlled and steered properly than to let it seek its own course. Positioning techniques are needed to project how a country is different and better than the competition.

There is, however, an added dimension to this situation. As with other world brands, the country identity may be seen differently in different areas of the world. Just as Coke has a different image in Moscow as opposed to London, so too will a country be viewed differently by people in different countries. For example, Country A may be seen very differently by Countries B, C, and D depending on the length of their relationship, the experiences they have shared, the depth of that relationship, and their distinctive cultures. Furthermore, even within Country B, C, or D, Country A will need to send different messages to different target audiences such as government, business, and media, making sure that over time perceptions change and the desired identity becomes reality in people's minds. Each country therefore has to do what companies do, which is to have a global identity and at the same time manage it locally.

An additional problem area for countries with regard to positioning is the need to balance short-term and long-term objectives and concerns. For instance, countries experiencing instability and investor confidence may have to cope with day-to-day attacks of reported bad news from national and domestic press, and yet still have the presence of mind to keep pushing out the positive messages which, although hard to justify currently, are vital for the longer term goal of building a strong image through influencing world opinion. This balancing act has to take place, but more often than not countries concentrate on the here and now and allow themselves to be forced by the media into defensive, reactive, and often negative statements. In such circumstances, it is even more important that countries project a continuous stream of positive messages that maintains the posture of confidence and optimism. Positioning must remain strong in the face of adversity. Central to this whole process, whether for a country, company, or person, is the ability to segregate the various target audiences and develop key messages for each of them.

Some countries such as Australia, Spain, and Chile have implemented large-scale campaigns to update their images in recent years. Others are determined to do so. Prime Minister Tony Blair is determined to bring about a change in the positioning of Britain. He wants to change the identity of UK PLC. But this is not just a whim; it is part of a range of strategies designed to help solve long-term problems facing Britain.

The image of Britain in the past has been strong, with respect to its achievements and reputation, but that age has now passed. The 'Great' in Great Britain has tended to fade out of people's perceptions around the world, and it no longer has the clear powerful identity it once enjoyed. Research reveals that Britain is perceived to be somewhat arrogant and aloof, not very innovative or competitive, rigid, backward looking, and generally dull and uninteresting. When compared to the rest of Europe, the United States, and Japan, it falls way behind on specifics such as quality, excellence, value for money, market leadership, innovation, and communications. Even with its own people, Britain has poor perceptions, which can be summarized in a lack of pride and respect for what Britain produces and what it stands for. Having a poor position in people's minds can adversely affect overall economic performance.

Peter Mandelson, when acting as Britain's Minister without Portfolio, said in 1997: 'A modernised, rebranded Britain is an essential condition to secure the investment, trade, jobs and prosperity we want to achieve for our country.' Some initiatives have already been taken, noting that global concerns still need to generate local messages that support overall positioning strategy, but build up local specific perceptions. In Malaysia, for example, Britain has developed a set of brand values and a positioning, backed by a major campaign involving public and private sector organizations, which caters for special relationship building with that country. Other initiatives are also underway in other Asian countries.

Nor is Britain the only nation facing an identity crisis—many developed and developing countries are confronting similar challenges. The crucial issue for any country is how they are perceived at home and particularly abroad. Perceptions, as we know, determine both position and image, and with countries perceptions are determined in the main by mass media. The challenge therefore is to counteract bad press and send out positive messages. This is made particularly difficult by the fact that the media tend to prefer reporting bad news rather than good news, because bad news sells more copies and attracts bigger audiences.

Individual countries have their own positioning problems. Those in South-East Asia have currency instability, a lack of investor confidence, misconceptions about various economic, political, and social issues, all of which are fuelled by bad press and inadequate perception management. Some countries are now realizing that the management of perceptions is the key to the restoration of international credibility and confidence and are trying to bring about a better positioning. Korea (South Korea) runs an advertisement on CNN sponsored by the country's Tourism Board showing scenic shots of the country, with the president saying 'Korea is changing ... Come and see the New Korea'.

Another Asian country is positioning itself through media advertisements as being different and better than any other. Taiwan (Republic of China) is saying that as the rest of the region struggles to overcome financial adversity, it alone is a haven of economic resilience, providing not just a guide for renewed growth and prosperity, but leadership in high-tech product expertise, helping to keep Asia connected to the future. It highlights its strengths and attributes, such as:
- Cutting-edge technology
- A world first in the production of notebook computers, scanners, modems and mouse accessories
- No undue reliance on short-term international debt
- Market freedom so that its entrepreneurs can innovate
- Agile small- and medium-sized businesses
- A strong 'node' in the Asia–Pacific network

All of these technology-based positions are summed up in the tag line 'Connected to the 21st Century', and the message 'Taiwan today is making a difference for Asia's tomorrow'. What Taiwan is trying to do is to convince people that it is better than other countries in Asia, such as Singapore, for technology companies. It does so by positioning itself on its greatest strength.

CHECKLIST FOR POSITIONING NATIONS

Countries and nations wishing to project a new identity and create a better image can benefit just as people and companies can by employing strategic positioning techniques, namely:
- Create a set of specific brand identity values.
- Capitalize on current brand equity (good perceptions).

- Clearly define all target audiences they wish to influence.
- Have a clear understanding of their current and desired perceptions.
- Clarify all perception gaps.
- Identify a national positioning strategy.
- Develop specific positioning strategies for each target audience.
- Create positive key messages for each target audience, on a continual basis.
- Develop a communications plan, including selection of appropriate media, to achieve objectives with each audience, covering global and local advertising and public relations campaigns.
- Ensure all government departments and senior politicians speak with one voice in projecting the values.
- Relate policies to positioning in presenting materials for media.
- Carry out ongoing research into target audience perceptions, and adjust messages accordingly.
- Ensure brand guardianship via the most appropriate mechanism.

It must be emphasized that creating identities and powerful positions for nations demands, as with companies and persons, real substance, as credibility and perceptual change need to be supported by actions, and not just promises or empty rhetoric.

Positioning and Country of Origin: Problems and Opportunities

Country of origin has been proved by research to be a key image attribute used by consumers in their positive or negative evaluations of products and brands. Some companies take advantage of the positive image and associations of their home countries to strengthen their identity and appeal. For example, Carlsberg always relates its products to Denmark, using the caption 'The original beer from the Danish Master Brewer', and the royal coat of arms on the packaging. Other companies say with some dismay that being associated with their country puts them at a disadvantage in their chosen markets. This depends to some extent on what the country is known for producing as well. For instance, it is easier to introduce a new watch product if your company is from Switzerland, but much more difficult if the company is from Myanmar.

However, in general, companies from the developed world find it relatively easy to strengthen their position with the country endorsement. With developed nations there seems to be a certain element of status that allows companies to use home associations, but with less developed countries even the indigenous populations prefer to buy foreign produce. Experienced China marketeers know well that Chinese consumers perceive significant differences between local and foreign brands, and scrutinize brands to a much greater extent than is common in more developed markets. This attitude is prevalent in many Asian countries, where international brands are seen to offer better quality and design, have better reputations and, while being more expensive, are still perceived to offer better value.

The economic turmoil is providing opportunities for some companies to take advantages of 'buy local' sentiments encouraged by governments wishing to reduce costly imports and encouraging local manufacturing for exports. In Malaysia a company called Sun Rhythm has introduced a Malaysian brand of toiletries, Kirei, in response to such encouragement, aimed at giving customers a choice of top quality made-in-Malaysia products. All the products carry the slogan 'Proudly Made in Malaysia'.

Internationally, country of origin is also a problem for Asian companies trying to position themselves in foreign markets. While common sense and textbooks tell us that it is product quality that makes for success, it is not the reality of the situation. Try to market products with the endorsements 'Made in China' or 'Made in Thailand' and success is not likely even though the quality can be of comparable standard to similar products made in Britain or the United States. The reality is that some of Asia's best companies struggle to gain a strong position and develop international brands because of the country of origin association. The lack of strong global brands in Asia is the result of this, the exception being Japan which struggled for a couple of decades or more to overcome such perceptions and is now seen as a developed nation making quality products. The initiative by Taiwan is a deliberate attempt to help its business sector overcome this positioning problem by repositioning the country itself.

Such pronounced consumer attitudes have a great deal to do with risk in terms of product performance, and the lesser the consumer familiarity with the brand is, the greater the risk is perceived to be. Famous brands are much less affected by the 'made in' labelling, as is the case of Nike's shoe manufacturing in Vietnam and other developing countries, and no one seems to care at all where Coke is made—the country of manufacture may visibly be China, Thailand, or elsewhere but the product still sells. The implication for established international brands or products is that they should take advantage of this valuable multicountry sourcing asset as long as their positioning is not hampered by unfavourable country of origin associations.

For those companies trying to market products where the country of origin association is less favourable, the options are fairly limited. They can:

1 Disguise the association, as the mineral water brand Minère did by labelling the bottle with the words 'France' and 'Perrier Vittel' while the country of origin (Thailand) connection was less visible on the contents label at the back. Distancing the product in such a way appears to be one viable solution. This particular example is sometimes called an anchoring strategy as the product is 'anchored' to French mineral water drinks. Some successful Asian companies have used this method also, such as Padini, a company producing and marketing various fashion products. Padini is a Malaysian company that has enjoyed tremendous success by producing a variety of brands under international sounding names. The Padini and Padini Authentics names cater for men's apparel. Then Vincci was introduced as a line of contemporary fashion accessories for women. Seed is a fashion line of clothing for young people, Miki Kids for children, and Miki Mom for mothers. The company travels the world to keep up with the latest global fashion trends, and the international type brand names have attracted fashion-conscious consumers who want such products at reasonable prices.

2 Form joint ventures or other strategic alliances that allow

production in a different country, thus allowing a more prestigious positioning and new country labelling.
3 Enter into mergers and acquisitions of companies engaged in the same business, which enable companies to completely hide the country of origin.
4 Sponsor international events and invest in celebrity endorsements to position the company and its products as globally acceptable.
5 Claim expertise in their chosen fields, as Ponds and Shiseido have done with research institutes, and so on.

GLOBAL AND LOCAL POSITIONING DECISIONS: GETTING THE RIGHT BALANCE

One decision that every company ambitious enough to want to penetrate international markets has to make is whether to go for local or global positioning. Many well-known global brands such as Coca-Cola, Nestlé, Gillette, Levi Strauss, and others have already taken the decision and have established themselves around the world with one powerful positioning. But there are arguments for both local and global positioning.

LOCAL POSITIONING

Local positioning, that is, producing specific strategies and even names for specific local markets, usually by country, has the following benefits:
- Names, logos, symbols, and other visual parts of the company or product identity can be developed locally.
- Product development can be tailored to local markets to suit local preferences.
- Marketing, advertising, and promotion strategies can be selected without the constraints of globally produced communications.
- The risk of 'buy local' demands are greatly reduced.

GLOBAL POSITIONING

Global positioning, on the other hand, brings an entirely different set of benefits, namely:
- Associations with the 'home' country
- Cost savings in advertising, promotion, and packaging

- Perceptions of a global presence, which include being seen as safe, reliable, world class quality
- Exposure to world markets with a better chance of a consistent image

However, global positioning must be carefully executed in every market in order to avoid any possible negative effects, such as names that might not be culturally acceptable.

This polarization of choices has led to the now well-known combinations embodied in the word *glocal*, where the company has a global product or company stance but tailors this in a variety of ways to the local markets it serves. Different companies approach this problem differently, and this depends to a large extent on the nature of their operations. For instance, companies manufacturing and marketing fast-moving consumer goods like Nestlé go to great lengths to adapt their brands to local conditions, with just about every brand strategy consideration except financial management which is being handled country by country. Country managers can even carry out their own research and product development, as well as be in control of segment focus, advertising, promotion, and even brand name in some cases.

Despite going to great lengths to locally adapt themselves to different cultures, the global branded companies do tend to stick with a core corporate positioning, even if they position their products with sensitivity. Soups are a specific example of where tailoring the products for a local taste is essential. Indeed soup manufacturers offer product variations for different segments within one market, recognizing and assessing the separate likes and dislikes of different groups of people, and positioning them appropriately. Companies like Campbells who make such products are nevertheless corporately consistent with their brand positioning.

At the other extreme, companies producing global business products such as Corning and Rolls Royce (television components and aircraft engines respectively) maintain a largely central control of their corporate and product brand positioning, but in reality they market universal products with a universal market which need little adaptation. In the middle are car manufacturers such as Honda and Toyota creating universal products and positioning them with relatively small technical and nomenclature modifications, as opposed to thoroughly tailoring and positioning models for each country.

Whatever the decisions taken in developing a *glocal* branding framework, strategic positioning is of the utmost importance. For the truly adaptive mode, every market and segment of the market are treated individually, and products have to appeal to each in different ways. This requires several distinctive positions. For the largely unadapted mode, a globally focused position designed to generate similar perceptions is the route. For those situations requiring *glocal* branding, the positioning task is to retain the perceptual advantages of a world brand with enough local thinking to ensure acceptance at the more micro level.

Because few companies are in a situation where they can globally standardize every brand element, the real positioning challenge with international branding is to achieve a balance between the need to create and maintain a consistent strategic position, with the requirement of adding perceived value to discerning and different markets. The giants have learned to do this well. McDonald's has global products and a global family positioning, but within this framework it caters for local cultural tastes with its menus. In India there are mutton, fish, chicken, and vegetarian options with no beef or pork. There is even a Maharaja Mac. Belgium, Iceland, and Holland have their own special sauces, and so on.

Another case in point is Disney's animated film *Mulan*, the heroine being a young Chinese girl who goes to war in the place of her old father. Most people think this would be ideally suitable for all typical Disney audiences, especially the Chinese. Research showed, however, that Taiwan and Hong Kong audiences did not take to it very easily, and mainland China has not made a decision on whether to allow the film to be shown or not. The answer to the problem is in positioning, says Disney, and the film is now being positioned as one of great pride to the Chinese people, with the heroine as a great lady who conquers the world. Reinforcing the position, posters in Taiwan had Mulan in a soldier's attire, and Hong Kong's movie star Jackie Chan features as the voice of one character. The reaction to this emotional, patriotic positioning has evidently been tremendously positive. Had Disney not been sensitive to the thinking of local audiences, the latest world product would undoubtedly been relatively unsuccessful by the company's standards.

The important implication for positioning then is that while companies can have global brands, the global consumer does not exist, and international positioning must take into account cultural differences.

INTERNATIONAL POSITIONING: SOME CONSIDERATIONS

If you are in a situation where you are moving a product or a brand into one or more countries, it is important to remember that perceptions will almost certainly differ, even if the same marketing mix is used. For instance, in Singapore and Malaysia, Ikea—the retailer of modern furniture often purchased by young married couples—has a slightly upmarket image, but in the United States it is regarded as a company selling products of relatively poor quality, while in the United Kingdom the products are seen as good value for money.

Additionally, values are also variable, especially between Asia and the West. So while Western countries value positioning that emphasizes individualism and achievement, in Asian countries the needs of society, the family, and group are placed before the person. In this case, products and brand positioning strategies would need to appeal more to a collective group, stressing the benefits accordingly.

Although there are some segments that have universal needs, youth for example, and some products and brands have universal appeal, such as jeans, it is not automatic that one positioning can carry across every market. Even global brands like Levi's have to modify their positioning to suit different countries. For example, play down sex in Asia, play up rebellion in Europe. On the other hand, power prestige brands like Cartier and Rolex can be perceived like powerful people, and so be treated with great respect.

However, things are changing. Figure 9.1 represents a shift in age group attitudes toward modern fashions and fast moving consumer goods. Within this type of grid, research will help you find out prevailing attitudes in different countries. Japan's youth are more sophisticated and fashion conscious, for instance, and traditional values are being eroded, especially

FIGURE 9.1
International Positioning: Shifts in Age Group Attitudes

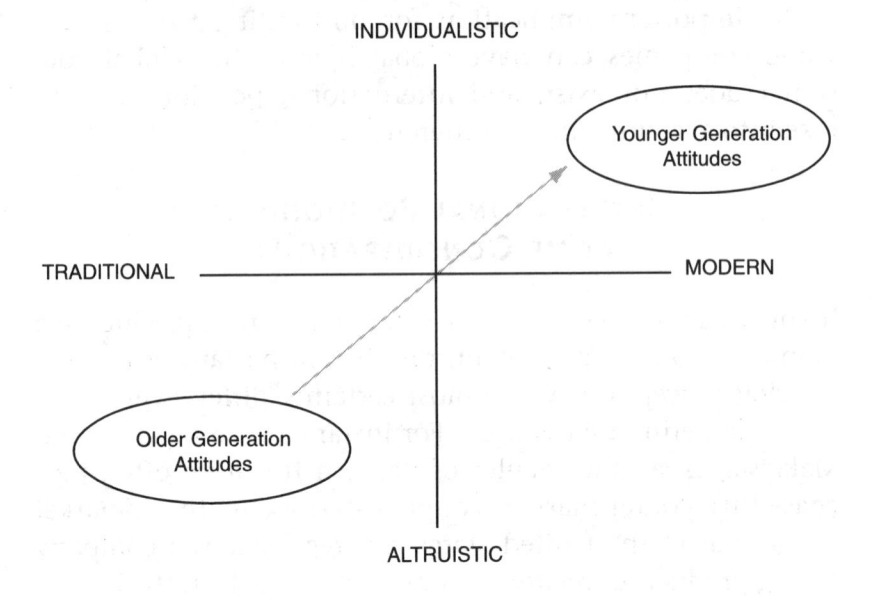

[Diagram: A two-axis chart with vertical axis labeled INDIVIDUALISTIC (top) and ALTRUISTIC (bottom), and horizontal axis labeled TRADITIONAL (left) and MODERN (right). An "Older Generation Attitudes" oval is in the bottom-left quadrant, and a "Younger Generation Attitudes" oval is in the top-right quadrant, with an arrow showing movement from older to younger.]

as the youth are increasingly exposed to Western brands. However, the rebellious youth is not yet an accepted norm. Other Asian countries, such as China and Indonesia, still uphold many traditional values, and although the youth are brand conscious, the segment has not moved into the top right quartile yet. This is of course influenced by many other factors such as religion and amount of disposable income, but the point is not this—it is that you cannot assume that universal segments behave or think the same from country to country. In fact, the more upwards the movement is to the right, the more volatile the markets and the more fickle the consumers are. The message is to exercise due care to understand your market thoroughly before moving from country to country, even in your own region.

Tough Choices in Positioning Technology

THE SPEED OF TECHNOLOGICAL DEVELOPMENT

Technological developments are occurring with frightening speed. With product life cycles shortening all the time—now a matter of weeks in many product categories, such as personal computers—great problems are posed for companies branding and positioning technology products. Brand managers are schooled in the 3 'C's of branding (consistency, consistency, consistency), but if they find themselves in any industry based on technology they now have to face a complete opposite set of 3 'C's (change, change, change). This will be the catch-22 of twenty-first century technology-based business. How can companies brand and position products to gain and maintain a good image—sending consistent messages to markets—and at the same time deal with the short-term sales pressures brought about by increasingly rapid obsolescence?

THE PSYCHOLOGY IS DIFFERENT WITH TECHNOLOGY PRODUCTS

There are also differences in the psychology of consumer behaviour when compared to that involved in the buying of normal consumer products. Consumer products in general are reasonably simple to understand in terms of features and benefits, whereas technology products are comparatively complex. With respect to the buying decision, people tend to be more impulsive with consumer products, but with technology products they exercise more care and consideration.

People also have overriding emotional issues of concern when trying to make decisions on which technology product to buy. These concerns are based on fear of not just how a particular product will perform, but also its parentage (brand identity). So in positioning technology products, there is a need to satisfy both the utilitarian needs of consumers and their emotional needs. This means that technology companies more than ever need to develop not just a respectable or reputable image, but strong relationships with consumers, and they must not forget that at the point of decision emotion sells.

Typical of the positioning stance taken by technology companies in trying to show that they are state-of-the-art and at the same time give comfort to risk-averse consumers is that recently exhibited in an advertisement by Applied Materials which has a headline of 'Total Innovation ... New ideas Don't Have to be Risky', followed by copy elaborating on this statement. Applied Materials also makes use of the problem—solution positioning strategy, linking its innovative characteristic to solving client problems. The problem—solution strategy can be used to introduce an emotional response, as demonstrated by Northern Telecom in one advertisement stating, 'Telecommunications markets are being deregulated around the world. Your competition is already positioned to reap the profits. There's a company that can help you get there first.' It goes on to explain how 'We'll help speed your success'.

Perhaps the most successful technology company to balance the dual requirements of innovation and reliability in its branding is Intel Corporation, as shown in the following case study.

CASE STUDY: INTEL CORPORATION

Because of the fears consumers have when things go wrong with technology products they react disproportionately. Take the well-documented example of Intel Corporation. As mentioned earlier, the initial faults discovered by customers after the launch of the Pentium chip by Intel were potentially devastating, and the company was receiving up to 10,000 calls a day from dissatisfied or unhappy customers. Good crisis management saved the day, and Intel regained their position of trust and high quality performance in the minds of consumers.

Intel is a model of good technology branding and positioning, and had it not already had a strong position, crisis management may not have been enough to save the day. The company really survived and prospered because of this, and has shown how a strategic positioning approach can solve the problems of consumer technophobia, with its now famous Intel Inside campaign. As a component that is not visible to consumers who buy personal computers, and original equipment manufacturers (OEM) offering price advantages to manufacturers, this was no easy task.

The Intel position has always been based on authenticity, quality, and performance, supported strongly by consistent global campaigns. The Intel Inside logo is placed on all print advertising, print and point-of-sale merchandising, shipping cartons, and packaging. It is also used by world brands and computer OEM. Supported by explanatory communication material, it has to a large extent succeeded in calming the fears of consumers who are doubtful of the performance of critical and complicated product elements they do not understand. The introduction of the Intel 'Bunnypeople characters' in astronaut-type attire in an attempt to humanize and add personality to product has not been so successful, being perceived by many as cold and impersonal.

Interestingly, Intel has now developed individual product brands, as is the case with the Pentium and Pentium II range. The rationale for this is that a name like Pentium (derived from the Greek word *pent* meaning five and alluding to the fifth generation of X86 computer chips) provides a kind of shorthand which is more meaningful to the consumer, summarizing the benefits more easily. Pentium II is positioned as a high performance product aimed at business and consumer users. In 1998, the Intel equivalent of a 'no frills' product range called Celeron was introduced, endorsed by the parental name, but meant for a different target audience. Celeron is positioned around value, compatibility, and quality, but the initial offering did not have a brilliant start. In 1999, Intel introduced Pentium III, an even more powerful performer.

It remains to be seen whether Intel has really understood the needs of different market segments, and whether or not the cheaper product can hold true to the position and associations that Intel has so single-mindedly projected over the last several years. Only time will tell if consumers will perceive the move as a more risky alternative, and if Celeron will devalue the position of the higher priced existing products. In the worst scenario, the different products might cannibalize each other's sales, and generate customer confusion. Intel intends to introduce more branded chips, and careful education of the consumer in this highly complex market will be essential to negate customer confusion and achieve successful brand positioning.

The Intimate Future: The Trend from Relationship Marketing to the Segment of One

WHAT IS RELATIONSHIP MARKETING?

The relationship marketing concept seems to be where marketing is heading. It has emerged mainly in the field of industrial and services marketing, but is supported by trends throughout modern business. Relationship marketing has been explained as establishing, maintaining, and enhancing relationships with customers and other partners, at a profit, so that the objectives of the parties involved are met. A mutual exchange and fulfilment of promises achieve this, and such relationships tend to be long term. They imply individual, or one-to-one relationships, and loyalty to a brand or company, and the process can be divided into attracting, then building and maintaining the relationship.

RELATIONSHIP MARKETING AND CUSTOMER LOYALTY

One of the most marked changes for companies and brands is the substantial decline in loyalty. Because of this, marketeers are now shifting their focus from customer acquisition to customer retention. They are doing this first because it is several times more expensive to gain a new customer than it is to keep an existing one. This is sheer economics, and with the current economic turbulence, the pressure is on for companies to reduce costs but still add value for the customer. The second reason that this trend is occurring is because a loyal customer not only generates retention cost advantages, but they tend to be the more frequent purchasers, and often act as advocates for the company or product. In other words, they are essential for the building of strong brands and long-term business growth.

Hence loyalty building is occupying a great deal of strategic marketing time, thought, and investment, with many corporate leaders pursuing this approach. John Pepper of Procter and Gamble is quoted on the first page of an annual report as saying that 'brand loyalty builds market leadership', and in pure monetary terms researchers are saying that increases in customer loyalty by only 5 per cent have brought about profit increases of up to 85 per cent!

Things Are What They Used To Be

The big question then is how to go about building customer loyalty? The answer is by building strong relationships with customers. This is of course not rocket science, and many will no doubt see an immediate link with the corner shop of yesteryear that used to sell most things that families required, knew all of the customers by name and their purchasing habits, and gave them very personal service. The companies that have replaced these outlets have now at last realized the value of getting to know and befriend the customer. Indeed, some of the giants of retailing are now actually trying to create and recreate this heritage with their own small dispersed outlets convenient to local communities, and offering more personal attention. So we find that relationship marketing attracts attention again in an old-fashioned way, and also in some sophisticated ways.

Relationship marketing in the old-fashioned way has never gone away. Alex, who has a small tailor shop in Kuala Lumpur, keeps all his customers measurements and clothing preferences on a small computer. He sends them notes to remind them to visit him on their next trip, and will work overnight if necessary to complete a suit order for a foreign visitor who has to depart the next day for another business destination, carrying out fittings and final delivery at the customer's hotel. This is unforgettable service. Relationship marketing relies on good products and services, but larger companies are finding other opportunities to tie in the customer for a long-lasting relationship, mainly in the area of monetary and non-monetary rewards.

RELATIONSHIP MARKETING: MODERN INTERPRETATIONS

Relationship marketing is probably one of those areas of modern business activity that is often least understood but widely discussed and attempted in various forms. Here are some of the concepts upon which it is based.

Customer Loyalty and the Parity Problem

Customer loyalty has declined at an alarming rate due to a proliferation of products and services in most categories. Customers have many choices and are more discriminating, having less loyalty, and showing relative indifference between two or three brands per category. Research carried out on fast-moving consumer goods shows that in many product categories they may have a slight preference for one particular brand, but in the event of its unavailability, they will not hesitate to choose another major brand from their 'repertoire'.

In many categories, products and services are at parity, and consumers see less and less differentiation between brand offerings. In other words, there is so much clutter nowadays that many product and service markets are packed with alternative choices for the public; they have become commodity markets. This is happening with increasing frequency, and it is a major challenge for positioning. For instance, in the airline industry there are a large number of players all offering the basic 'nuts and bolts' of flying. Customers book their tickets, arrive at the airport, check in, wait, spend a certain amount of time 'in the tube', and then safely disembark at their destination. Fundamentally, it is a commodity market driven by prime needs in the form of routes, timing, class configuration/seat availability, pricing, and certain standards of ground handling efficiency, punctuality, and in-cabin service. When customers consider these factors a number of airlines will meet their requirements. How do customers differentiate between them? When the basic qualifying factors are in place and the consumer is considering options, then image and relationships come into play, and this is where positioning expertise can make the all important difference. British Airways and other companies are now spending vast amounts of money on relationship marketing programmes, to position themselves in such a way that they can attract and retain customers.

Only the world brands command real loyalty, and even they are having to work very hard to keep it. Adidas is taking market share away from giants Nike and Reebok, and other companies are moving in. There will be no safe havens for any corporations in the next century, and the real battleground will be not products and services but managing perceptions and relationships. Failure to win this battle will result in decreased margins, customer migration, and lack of profitability.

Customer Profitability

Research has now proved beyond doubt the economic impact of long-term relationships with customers on profitability. Companies now are often involved in calculating the lifetime value of a customer. FedEx, for example, encourages its sales people to look at the value of one transaction with one customer, and what that value or worth might be if the customer repeats that transaction once a month, say for ten or even twenty years. This puts the relationship in a completely new perspective, and suggests a serious need for a strategy to achieve it.

Customer Equity

Companies have realized that relationships with customers develop 'equity'. The more you can add value to the customer relationship, then the greater that 'equity' will be. This is really a part of brand equity, but the realization that it can be built up quickly and focused upon as a separate entity is fairly new. As a part of brand equity, it naturally adds value to the overall worth of a brand or company, and can be a powerful leverage in mergers and acquisitions, even being valued by some companies as an asset in the balance sheet. So relationship marketing has a role to play in both balance sheet and profit and loss terms.

Rational and Emotional Dimensions

Relationship marketing has incorporated in its execution the bicameral aspects of the brain, recognizing that relationships are built on emotions and feelings as opposed to logic and rationality. It adds emotion to marketing strategy because its execution is very personal, makes people feel important, and gives them the glow of personal attention that they crave in this increasingly technological world. Positioning is the means of achieving this.

Corporate Personality

The new strategic initiatives of companies who are trying to generate a unique corporate personality, as described in the book *Corporate Charisma* (Temporal and Adler, 1998), reinforce the idea that relationships and the personalities with whom customers develop relationships are important. Companies are increasingly trying to become 'friends' with consumers, and relationship marketing is therefore a good route to take.

The bottom line for marketing then is that customers are not just wanting, but demanding individual treatment. Relationship marketing is the corporate response to a multitude of shifting consumer attitudes that culminate in programmes designed to capture and keep the individual customer. It is not a desperate response, but it is a compelling one that cannot be excluded from the marketing mix. It cannot succeed without thoughtful and well-executed positioning.

Which Customers Do We Want?/Which Customers Want Us?

Having said all this, relationship marketing sensibly does not target every customer, and the notion of the high-value customer (HVC) has not been forgotten. So some effort is always put into discovering who are the profitable customers, and who are not. The sophistication of technology can provide this information now with relative ease, and give more precision to the old 20/80 rule, valuable though it still may be in giving approximations. The average customer might spend US$6, but 20 per cent of customers might spend US$70 and 80 per cent spend only US$1, so it is no good looking at averages.

Profitability per customer is still a major issue, and in many companies still an unknown factor. So questions must be asked such as:

- Who are our high-value customers?
- Who are the potential high-value customers?
- What is the relationship between frequency of purchase and profitability?
- What are the opportunities to extend the purchase portfolio of these customers?

- Who are our low-value customers?
- How can we get them to become mid- to high-value customers? If we cannot, is the cost of keeping them worthwhile? And above all....
- How can we induce all the customers we really want to stay with us, and buy more from us?

Looking at a customer base in this way can provide astonishing insights. Tesco, for instance, found that the bottom 25 per cent of customers represented only 2 per cent of sales, and the top 5 per cent represented 20 per cent. They also found that the top 100 customers were worth the same as the bottom 4000. Tesco now measures valuable customers by frequency of purchase and value of expenditure, and allocates a great proportion of the time and money it spends on its customer loyalty programmes on the techniques of strategic positioning and perception management.

The key to relationship marketing is knowing your customers, and their value, and involving them in what the company is doing. This is influencing positioning practice.

RELATIONSHIP MARKETING TRENDS

Some of the trends given impetus by relationship marketing are:
- Interactive Advertising
- Relationship-building Promotions
- Customer Loyalty Programmes
- Database Marketing
- Direct Marketing
- Personality Strategies

These are described briefly below.

Interactive Advertising

Interactive advertising involves asking people to respond—take a direct action—and experience the relationship with a company or product. Whether to get more information (Flora Margarine), have a chat (Prudential Assurance), or relate your first experience of a new product (Coca-Cola OK), the important factor is involvement. Not just involvement for the sake of it, but to exchange value and develop a powerful relationship positioning in people's minds.

British Airways enjoyed a major success with 'The World's Biggest Offer' campaign. Its purpose was to revive flagging sales following the Gulf War and create a valuable customer database. With 5 million responses in 10 days giving the airline details of entrants and what they wanted from travel, the campaign was an unqualified success, all achieved through direct response advertising.

Relationship-building Promotions

Historically, promotions have not enjoyed a good reputation. They have sometimes been blamed for reducing value in the minds of customers, and being merely tactical with short-term benefit only. Generally, they have not been used for relationship building. However, if correctly targeted and used in a more strategic way to get customers to stay with the product over time, they can be effective.

Customer Loyalty Programmes

If relationship marketing focuses on the lifetime value of customers, then clearly customer loyalty is of the utmost importance. There is certainly a trend now towards not just customer acquisition but customer retention, and to be able to retain customers, companies must continue to add value to the customer relationship. True loyalty results not just in repeat purchase, but also advocacy and brand association. The value added comes from the strength of the relationship-building process, which in turn is dependent on positioning expertise.

Database Marketing

Relationship marketing is a continuous process dealing with each individual. The more that is known about each individual, the easier it should be to create the relationship, and so strategic database marketing is now a major field of activity in its own right and involves:
- Identifying specific customers or prospects
- Communicating with them
- Capturing the resulting information
- Using that information to further build the relationship and secure the desired image.

It is claimed that companies using database marketing could track 50 million customers individually, and all at a reasonable cost. Techniques have become so sophisticated that marketeers can now get to know all their customers on a one-to-one basis, just like the way shopkeepers of yesteryears used to do.

Database marketing in the next century will have increasingly more information on the customer. Apart from the usual demographic data, companies can now easily find out who has recently purchased their products and those of competitors. They can relate all this data to psychographics and financial information to provide detailed pictures of how individuals and families live, and the relationships they have. Much of this data has been around in one form or another for some time, but it is the new powerful database technologies that make the organization and interpretation of it possible.

In the not so distant future, more extensive data will exist on personality types and thinking styles which will enable relationship marketeers to move another huge step towards predicting consumer behaviour, managing perceptions, and maintaining powerful dialogues and positions.

Direct Marketing

Direct marketing combines database management with one or more media to achieve a transaction or another type of response. While it is intended to be personal it is sometimes misused, and more often than not it is regarded by customers as junk mail. It is more costly per customer contact than normal advertising but for audiences of 300,000 or less it can be very effective. Nowadays direct marketing also includes the Internet, smartcards, and in some countries interactive television. It clearly represents a powerful tool for use in relationship marketing, as its main aim is to bring customers closer to the company and its products. Its implication for positioning is that understanding the differences between various market segments, and delivering the right messages to them is crucial.

Personality Strategies

A relationship marketing strategy gives companies the opportunity to use the power of corporate or product personality to strengthen and help customer bonding. Careful matching of corporate and brand communications to carefully chosen groups of people through positioning techniques can bring about a matching of personality types that can lead to true and lasting friendship, as explained in Chapters 5 and 8.

RELATIONSHIP MARKETING AND THE SEGMENT OF ONE

The ideal form of relationship is, of course, where the company can deal with each customer as an individual, and there is a growing trend towards making this happen. Here are a few examples of how companies are bringing in relationship marketing programmes that position themselves and their products and services more closely towards individual customers.

1. A clothing company in the United States is using mass customization technology by introducing a body scanner that can isolate over 300,000 body points using 6 cameras and light patterns that create 48 video photos. The result is that consumers can be fitted with clothing that exceeds their expectations of the transaction. The company had realized that over half of people who by ready-made clothes do not fit well into standard sizes. In addition to making the customer happy, the device could shorten production cycles down to forty-eight hours. Similar technology is already in use in Europe and Japan, and Levi Strauss (a leader now in made-to order clothing) says that in the near future a large percentage of its products will either be made to order or sold direct to customers.
2. National Semiconductor is focusing on its most valuable costumer accounts with its launch of fifty private web sites in 1998 to cater for their customers' special needs and wants. The company uses these web sites to send customized sales messages and other proprietary information such as product specifications, contract pricing, project status reports, and customer support information that will help develop better customer relationships.
3. American Airlines' web site now has new features to assist one-to-one interactions and transactions, based on individual preferences and past interactions. Each customer profile will contain hundreds of pieces of information from nearest airport to frequent destinations, a new form-free booking process, plus updates on special offers. This

relationship initiative is intended to enhance customer loyalty.
4. The well-known toy brand Fisher-Price has a new web site with personal shopper features, such as a search for gifts based on age, gender, price, and toy type. Results give photos and retail locations. Parents expecting the birth of a child get their e-mail orders supplied by mail which includes a handbook of advice.
5. Financial services firm Piper Jaffray's Equity Capital Markets division has customers who are CEOs, stock analysts, and portfolio managers, to whom time, speed, and accuracy of information are precious. It has brought in a relationship marketing database that gives a view of each customer's preferences and needs, enabling it to precisely deliver the right information at the right time.
6. United Airlines top frequent fliers often get a handwritten card from the captain of the plane thanking them for being one of United's best customers.
7. Motorola has re-engineered production of pagers to offer 256 options. Information technology matches the customer's order with the production process, and the pager is produced and shipped within one hour.

All of the above examples are illustrations of how companies are positioning themselves in ways which try to create the perception of friendship and individual attention for customers which will result in long-term relationships. These examples, and many others, can be found by going to the Internet site of Don Peppers and Martha Rogers (PeppersAndRogers@1to1.com). The Peppers and Rogers Group is regarded as the pioneer of one-to-one marketing, a leadership position they have built not just by writing about this important trend, but by doing it themselves and helping other companies to do the same.

POSITIONING IN TIMES OF ADVERSITY

CRISIS OR OPPORTUNITY

Industries and companies do not always enjoy good times. Markets change, competition and substitution can erode advantages held, and complacency can lose customers. Favourable positions can all too easily be lost. In such circumstances, the real need, which is to carefully think through how repositioning can effectively take place, is often ignored in the face of panic-driven, impulsive short-term thinking and decision making aimed at damage control to sales and profits. Similar situations can affect countries on a very large scale. For example, since mid-1997 much of Asia has been in deep crisis, and most of the world is affected economically by this situation. The question thus arises of whether or not it is wise or worthwhile to put more or less effort (and hence financial resources) into branding and positioning activities. The majority of companies appear to regard this recessionary period as a sign to cut down on this type of expenditure, while the minority see it as a window of opportunity for strategic investment.

Perhaps both views can be accommodated, but to stop investing in brands and their positioning would without doubt be detrimental to future success, for the following reasons:

1 There will always be one or more competitors that continue to invest in maintaining and strengthening their position and image, and those of their brands. To allow them to move ahead in this way will cause performance problems for organizations that do not take this strategic view and respond similarly.

2 Investing in positioning strength and image should be seen in the same way as investment in plant and capital equipment. Doing so keeps a firm up-to-date, at the cutting edge of the industry, and brings high returns on investment. Brands and image are valuable assets and have to be strengthened and revitalized as time goes by. Failure to revitalize these assets results in loss of brand equity, not just in terms of all the time and money that has been put into the image creation process previously, but also in terms of customer perception.

3 A strong image depends on a powerful positioning that keeps a presence in the minds of those people whom you want to influence. Like keeping a parking lot for a car, or renting an apartment, payment is required to keep a position in peoples' minds, to remind them we are there and to keep them loyal to us. It is particularly dangerous to cease paying 'mind rental' in those industries and categories

where loyalty and consumer preferences are weak, and where situations of parity exist or are developing. This is the situation in many markets today.

Given situations of economic recession and downturn, however, there is no escaping the fact that costs may have to be reduced all round including the marketing function, but it is possible to reduce expenditure on positioning activities without losing impact in the market-place. This can be achieved by:

- Advertising and promoting lower ranges of your product portfolio if you have them, to offset sales losses in the higher range, as some airlines are doing with economy class
- Introducing new products at the lower end
- Focusing on higher income customer groups who are not so affected by recessionary times
- Using less expensive forms of advertising (for example, the Internet, substituting print for television, reducing the length of commercials, or producing 'no frills' advertising)
- Using more direct marketing techniques
- Using more self-liquidating promotions
- Establishing loyalty programmes
- Establishing better management of customer relationships through internal culture change programmes
- Focusing on high value customers with customer relations management schemes
- Concentrating more on key messages that stress real strategic competitive advantages
- Co-branding and positioning to share marketing costs

CUTTING DOWN ON EXPENDITURE: DANGERS TO BE AWARE OF

When you are under pressure to reduce costs and increase sales, it is easy to forget some of the fundamentals that can both drive and destroy a good market position and image. For example, before being tempted into giving away price reductions, consider carefully the following implications:

- Will this alienate existing customers who previously bought at a higher price?
- Will your image suffer by suddenly offering 'cheap' promotions?

- Will you be able to revert to normal pricing in good times, or will you lose business through such a move?

It is important to understand your customer base, what their associations and perceptions are, and what tolerance levels they have. If you intend to introduce a new lower end product, do you really understand what the target audience wants, and will it fit into your portfolio without detracting from your current image? And if you intend to try co-positioning with other companies, are they a good fit for your image? These and other questions need to be answered with care before action is taken.

Whatever choices are made, it must be remembered that to strengthen and manage customer perceptions, frequency of communication is vital. Those that reduce communications substantially will damage their position and image.

Strategic Positioning: Points to Ponder

IMAGE DEVELOPMENT AND PROTECTION

This final section of the book is a reminder of what has been said, and takes the form of a checklist of questions you can use in creating a powerful position and image, and in protecting it from being weakened by competitor activity and neglect. The most important thing you must remember is that strategic positioning depends entirely on your ability to manage perceptions. The strategic positioning process outlined below takes you through all the steps necessary to create the right kind of perceptions in the minds of your target audience. However, positioning is not just a one-time activity; rather, it is a continuous process which needs constant attention if you want to maintain an overall perception of being different and better than the competitors. In fact, vigilance is essential to keep on top of perception management and maintain a strong image, because attacks on image can come in various forms, some of which are:

- Changes in competitor positioning strategies
- Escalation of competitor communications
- New companies, products, and services
- Disasters, crises, and rumours
- Changes in competitor positioning strategies
- Decreases in customer loyalty
- Changing patterns of market segment behaviour
- Decreasing product life cycles
- Deterioration in ability to deliver on promises
- Failure to keep up with technological change and industry developments

Managing perceptions through strategic positioning will provide solutions to these problems, by preparing for and deflecting attacks. The management of perceptions is the only way to achieve positioning success because it influences the thoughts of the people who really count—actual and potential customers. In marketing textbooks there are several 'P's that are part of the means of achieving visions, missions, and objectives, but at the end of the day the only 'P' that counts is perception, and the only vehicle for the governance of perceptions is strategic positioning.

This book has concentrated on showing you how to develop a powerful positioning that will give rise to a strong image. The principles are applicable to any image issue faced by a company, product, service, nation, place, or individual. Here then are the steps you should take when you are building an image, and a list of appropriate questions to ask at every stage.

Step 1: Taking a Good Look at the Market

The first step is to determine the precise war zone, and what is happening in it. Questions you should ask include:
- What business are you in?
- How fast is the market growing?
- What category of business are you in?
- Who are your main competitors for each product and service?
- What segments exist in the market you are interested in?
- Where are the growth opportunities? Which segments are growing faster than others are and why?
- Why do customers come to you/leave you?
- Why do they go to each of your competitors?
- What are your priorities for business growth?
- What target audience is the most important to you *now*? Have you defined it clearly enough?

Step 2: Understanding Your Present Image and Position

In this step it is time to get to grips with the perceptions of the target audiences you want to impress and influence. In this case, you will need answers to questions such as:
- How do people (employees and customers) see you at present?
- What are the good and bad aspects of your current image?
- How does your image compare with those of your key competitors?
- What are the main things that customers want to see in your type of enterprise? What are they looking for?
- What is the self-concept of your target customer, and how well can you fit that profile?
- What is your position relative to the competition on a consumer perceptual map?
- How close or far away from the consumer ideal preferences are you and the other players?
- What strategic opportunities are there to move into spaces or gaps that consumers would appreciate, and yet have not been filled?

- Can you do more research to add precision to these views of consumer perceptions?

Step 3: Developing Positioning Alternatives

Here the issue is how you are going to establish your desired image and position by searching through the various alternative strategies available. You must ask:

- What is your desired position and image?
- What space do you want to move into in the mind map of consumers?
- What strategy or combination of strategies do you think are best suited to achieving your goal?
- How are you going to explain what you stand for in terms of your personality, and what makes you both different and better than the main competitors?
- Are the options sustainable in the long run or will they only afford you a short-term differential advantage?
- Are they profitable enough?

Step 4: Testing Out the Positioning Strategy Options

At this stage the optional positions with the target audience you are pursuing must be tested out. This should involve some of the methodologies referred to earlier in the text, particularly focus groups. The aim is for you to find out not just whether or not they like what they see and hear, but also whether they will 'buy it'. The response from the people you ask must demonstrate that they would take action in moving towards you and away from competitors.

Step 5: Creating the Final Desired Position

Now it is time to write the final positioning statement, which should be phrased as far as possible in consumer language, as a proclamation of what precisely you want them to think. The mechanics of writing positioning statements are dealt with in Chapter 6, but they must contain answers to the following questions:

- What business or product class are you in?
- Who is your target audience?
- What benefits are you offering them?
- Why are you better than and different from the competitors?
- Are all your key messages clearly represented in the statement?

Above all, the desired position and image you wish to create in people's minds must be credible, believable, relevant to them, and capable of being delivered.

Step 6: Adapting to the New Position

At this stage, you have to decide on the best means of delivering the promise of the new position, and the implications this might have in terms of corporate and product formulation and change. Typical questions include:

- Do you have to develop a new product or adapt existing ones?
- Do you have to change your service standards?
- Do you have to change your visual identity, or product packaging?
- Do you have to change your brand name(s) or personality?
- Do you have to change your corporate culture or personality?
- Do you have to adjust your pricing or distribution policies?
- What will be your communications strategy once all these things are in place?
- When will all the necessary changes be in place so that the new positioning can be launched?

Step 7: Developing and Executing the Communications Plan

While the above changes are being put in place, you have to create a media plan that will communicate the new positioning to the target audience from the options described in Chapter 6. Relevant questions include:

- What communications media are you going to use?
- Does the plan integrate advertising, promotion, direct marketing, sponsorship, and public relations into consistent key messages with enough frequency?
- Are the campaigns durable enough to make an impact on perceptions and image?
- Is the personality reflected strongly, consistently, and appropriately enough in all creative execution?
- Is there a good balance of appeal to the rational and emotional sides of people's minds?
- How do the campaigns stack up against those of the competitors? Are they different and better?
- Has creative advertising been pretested, and if so, did it delight the sample audience?
- Do you know how you are going to track the effectiveness of the campaigns?

Step 8: Monitoring Success—Have You Achieved the Image You Want?

This last step is very important as you may have to adjust what you offer, your communications, or even your position if the desired impact is not there, if the market situation changes, or the perceptions, needs, and wants of the consumers evolve. Some questions for you to consider here are:

- How effective were the various elements of the communications campaign?
- Did they result in increased sales as well as awareness? Were they cost effective?
- Do consumers see you differently than before?
- Has the positioning effort been effective in gaining the desired space on perceptual maps?
- Are you closer to the consumer segment ideal points on preference maps?
- Is your positioning closer to the self-image of the consumer?
- Have your competitors changed positions? If so, what will your response be?
- Should you be concentrating now on positioning yourself for other segments?
- Do you need to strategically move into any new product areas to strengthen your whole category position?

Monitoring and measuring image and positioning means that you have to constantly evaluate every one of the steps mentioned above. If you do not do this, there is a real danger that you will lose touch with the market and, importantly, consumer feelings and perceptions. Image building is a continuous process and requires continuous feedback from all quarters. There is no room for complacency as corporate graveyards are littered with failed businesses that never understood the thoughts of those people who really counted. Images are fragile, delicate things that must be given care and attention. They exist only as thoughts and feelings, and temporarily occupy positions in people's minds. Without constant reinforcement and improvement they will lose their importance, and will be replaced by other, more strongly projected images. The strategic positioning process builds strong images, but it is careful management of the positions created that sustains them. Strategic positioning needs the discipline of constant information gathering, and guardianship to make sure that all activities that have an impact on perceptions are true to the desired image.

Strategic Positioning: Ten Points to Remember

There are ten points that must never be forgotten if you are to be successful in establishing a powerful position in people's minds.

1. Know your target audience.
2. Make your company, product, and/or service relevant to them.
3. Occupy the high ground of emotional and rational appeal.
4. Ensure the position clearly states why you are different to and better than the competitors.
5. Develop a communications strategy that portrays the positioning in a consistent, appropriate, and coherent manner.
6. Make sure you can deliver on the promise of the positioning.
7. Go for the long term and show your commitment.
8. Continually track the perceptions of your audience.
9. Change your position *only* if you really believe consumers will benefit from it.
10. Be courageous in protecting and guarding your positioning strategy and its execution.

Index

ABSOLUT VODKA, 133
Adidas, 190
Advertising, 132; and aspiration, 137; and drama, 135; and emotion, 133; and fear, 136; and humour, 136; and music, 137; and sex, 137; and shock, 136; and warmth, 137; execution, 150
Agency brief, 148
Air Lanka, 145
American Airlines, 196
American Express, 139
Armani, Georgio, 67
Analogies and metaphors, 167; see also Positioning success tracking
ASEAN Free Trade Area, (A.F.T.A.), 108
Attention, 3,4
Avon, 43

BASIC POSITIONING PROCESS, 24–6
B.A.T. Industries, 113
Baywatch, 32
Beckham, David, 58
Benetton, 43, 136
Bentley, 62
Blair, Tony, 74, 174
Blue Nun, 69–70
Boxer, Joe, 136
BUPA International, 134
Body Shop, 43
Borders, bookstore, 123–4
Brands, and branding, 73–9; 3 C's, 185; attitude, 16; awareness, 16; country of origin, 177; differentiation, 100; equity 43, 99; esteem, 100; knowledge, 100; power, 42; relevance, 100; revitalize, 61; stature, 100; strength, 100
Brand Asset Valuator, 99, 100
Brand guardianship, 96–7
Brand identity, 75–6
Brand image, 75–6
British Airways, 102–4,
British Broadcasting Corporation, 58
British Rail, 55
British Telecom (BT), 35
Brylcreem, 58

BSN Commercial Bank, 7
Bush, George, 17

CABLE NEWS NETWORK, (CNN), 67, 176
Cadbury, 87, 113
Carey, Mariah, 85
Canon, 38
Casio, 64, 88
Carat Club, 51–2
Carlsberg, 139, 177
Carizon, Jan, 112
Carrefour, 44
Cartier, 143, 183
Celeron, 187
Chan, Jackie, 182
Chanel, 61
Chronography, 167; see also Positioning success tracking
Citibank, 139, 143
Chrysler, 49, 50
Clapton, Eric, 66
Club Med, 112
Co-branding, 93–6; see also Brands and branding
Coca-Cola, 17, 38, 74
Colgate, 21, 74
Compaq, 74
Competitor positioning, 62; see also Repositioning
Concorde, 21, 74
Consumer behaviour, 40
Consumer opinion: influence of, 6
Copperfield, David, 19
Corning, 181
Corporate personality, 52, 192; revitalized, 60
Credit cards, 28, 116
Crisis management, 141
Customer equity, 191
Customer loyalty, 43; programmes, 194
Customer profitability, 191

DATABASE MARKETING, 194
Dell, 74, 110, 138
Dennis, Ron, 94
Dentsu, Young & Rubicam, 100
Dion, Celine, 85
Difference statements, 166

Differentiation, 51; see also Carat Club; Positioning strategies
Direct marketing, 138, 195; see also Marketing communications
Disney, 94, 182
Dockers, 89, 112; see also Levi Strauss
Docklands, 18
Don Peppers and Martha Rogers, 197
Dubai, 18
Dukakis, Michael, 17
Dulux, 40
Dunhill, Alfred, 39
Dylan, Bob, 66

EASTMAN KODAK, 94
Electronic business, 110, 111; see also Positioning strategies
Emotional phraseology, 50; see also Positioning strategies
Emotional Value, 44; see also Positioning strategies
Equity Capital Markets, 197

FED EX, 74, 191
Fidelity, 134
Fisher-Price, 197
Focus groups, 155–7; see also Research techniques
Ford Motor Company, 109
Four Seasons Hotel, the, 135, 145
Frito Lay, 94
Fujitsu, 107

GALANT, 68
Guinness, 65, 66, 81, 138

HÄAGEN-DAZS, 45
Haakinen, Mika, 94
Hard Rock Café, 74, 115
Harley-Davidson, 86
Heinz Tomato Ketchup, 131
Hewlett-Packard, 94, 113
Hilfiger, Tommy, 67
Hoechst, 134
Honda, 181
Hospitality industry, 22
Hovis, R.H.M., 63, 137
Hypercompetition, 4; see also Positioning strategy

IBM, 34, 35, 48, 74, 94
Ikea, 44
Intel Corporation, 94, 186, 187
Interactive advertising, 193; see also Relationship marketing
Image, 3; crafted, 19; of countries, 17; technically efficient, 61

JACKSON, MICHAEL, 19, 62, 66
John, Elton, 66
Johnson and Johnson, 45
Johnson Baby Shampoo, 50, 86
Jordan, Michael, 42, 91

KELLOG'S CORNFLAKES, 63
King, Larry, 19
Kit Kat, 39, 74
Klein, Calvin, 87
KLM, 145

LAURA ASHLEY, 60
Levi Strauss, 89, 112, 180
Leno, Jay, 19
Life cycle compression, 109; see also Positioning strategy
Lombard Odier, 134
Loyalty segmentation, 92; see also Brands and branding; Positioning strategy
Lucozade, 59

MADONNA, 57, 62, 74
Maggi noodles, 39
Mahathir Mohamad, 8
Maharaja Mac, 182
Mandelson, Peter, 175
Maradona, 91
Marlboro, 28, 77, 78, 81
Marketing communications, 125–50
Market penetration strategy, 45; see also Positioning strategy
Market segmentation and positioning, 115; see also Positioning strategy
Marks & Spencer, 44
Marriage/partnership choices, 167; see also Positioning success tracking
Mars, 45, 59
Mass customization, 122; see also

Positioning strategy; Strategic positioning
Mattel, 141
McCartney, Paul, 66
McDonald's, 23, 44, 94, 182
Mercedes Benz, 42, 78, 87, 88, 94
Microsoft, 33
Midland Bank, 39
Milo, 77, 80
Mind map, 205
Mental process, 5, 6; mental image, 21
Mitsubishi Motors, 68–9
Mission statements, 7, 8, 9
Motorola, 7; Iridium, 49; six sigma quality programme, 8
Mulan, 182
Multi-positioning, 86–9

NATIONAL SEMICONDUCTOR, 196
Nations: positioning of, 173–80
NatWest Bank, 40
Neon California, *see* Chrysler
Nestlé, 38, 42, 45, 80, 94, 180, 181
Nike, 40, 41, 49, 58, 86, 137, 190
Nissan cars, 94
No Frills, 44
Northern Telecom, 186

OBITUARY SKETCHING, 165; *see also* Positioning success tracking
One-to-one interviews, 162; *see also* Research techniques
One-to-one marketing, *see* Relationship marketing
One-to-one relationships, *see* Relationship marketing
Oracle, 35, 94
Orient Express, 21

PADINI, 179
Pangkor Laut, 18
Pentium, 187
Pepper, John, 188
Perceptions, 4, 5, 9; as reality, 56; automatic, 5; control or shape, 6; defined, 5; of competitors, 26; selective, 6; vehicle of governance, 203
Perceptual mapping, 153, 159, 160; *see also* Research techniques

Permodalan Nasional Berhad, 7
Perrier, 62
Perrier Vittel, 179
Personality, 3; basis of, 10; characteristics, 47; strategies, 48, 195; traits, 10
PGA Tour, 137
PHARMACY restaurant, 115
Photo sorting, 166; *see also* Positioning success tracking
Pictures/collages, 165; *see also* Positioning success tracking
Piper Jaffray, 197
Positioning, 11, 15, 26, 33, 34, 42, 45, 46, 84, 144, 163, 173, 177, 180, 184; definition, 5; evolutionary, 67–8; global, 180–3; international, 183–4; link to perception, 5; local, 180; revolutionary, 66–7; tools, 23
Positioning and image: the virtuous circle, 27
Positioning success tracking, 163–9
Positioning statements, 127; key messages, 130; writing and using, 129
Positioning strategy, 5; strategies, 31–52; world market trends affecting, 107–11; *see also* Strategic positioning
Power Grid, 99–101
Preference mapping, 161–2; *see also* Research techniques
Presley, Elvis, 74
Procter and Gamble, 98
Product diversity, 109; *see also* Positioning strategy
Proton cars, 40
Prudential Assurance, 193
Psychographics, 119; *see also* Research techniques; Strategic positioning
Public relations, 139; in crisis management, 141–2; *see also* Marketing communications

RAFFLES HOTEL, 78
Recalled experiences, 166; *see also* Positioning success tracking
Reebok, 190
Relationship marketing, 188–97;

and customer loyalty, 188–90; modern interpretations, 189–93; and segment of one, 196–7; trends, 193–6
Repositioning, 51, 53–70; eight major reasons, 55; multiple repositioning, 65; of nations, 173; repositioning the competition, 64
Research, qualitative, *see* Research techniques
Research, quantitative, *see* Research techniques
Research agencies, 146
Research techniques, 153–69
Richard, Cliff, 66
Ritz-Carlton hotel group, 31
Rolex, 42, 64, 78, 88, 143, 183
Rolling Stones, 66
Rolls-Royce, 20, 42, 62, 181

SALES PROMOTION TECHNIQUES, 139–9; *see also* Marketing communications
Scandinavian Airline System, (SAS), 70, 112
Schwab, Charles, 36
Segmentation process, 117; lifestyle segmentation, 121; recent trends, 118
Selective perception, 6
Self-image and attribute matching; 164; *see also* Positioning success tracking
Sheldon, Mike, 69
Singapore Airlines, 145
Singapore Telecom, 149
Sony, 36, 38
Spice Girls, 65
Sponsorships, 142
Standard Chartered Bank, 94
Stanford Research Institute, 119
Strategy, 32, 33, 34, 35, 36, 37, 41, 44
Strategic positioning: benefits of, 27–8; concept of, 1–26; issues, 171–200; and marketing communications, 125–50
Sun Rhythm, 178
Sustainable competitive advantage, 85; *see also* Brands and branding; Positioning strategy
Swatch, 64, 94

TAG HEUER, 61, 85, 143
Tag lines, 144; *see also* Marketing communications
Technology: positioning of, 184–7
Telebanking, 33
Telekom Malaysia, 35
Thatcher, Margaret, 16, 17
Toyota, 181

UNILEVER, 45
Unique selling proposition (USP), 34, 85, 109
Unisys, 55

VALUES, 10; core values, 63; a mindset, 45; rediscovering lost values, 62
Values and Lifestyles (VALS), 119
Vincci, 179
Virgin Airlines, 79
Virtual banking kiosks, 33
Vision, 7; customer-based information, 9; direction, 10; public statement, 8; written, 9
Vision 2020, 8
Volkswagen, 44
Volvo, 32, 136, 143

WALKMAN, 36
What if's, 166; *see also* Positioning success tracking
Woods, Tiger, 42, 137
World Trade Organisation (WTO), 107

YUPPIES, 26, 108